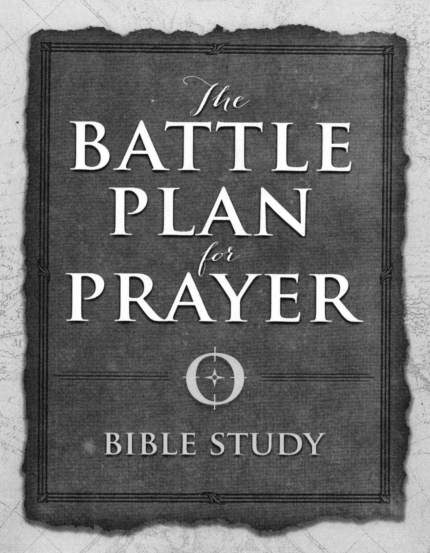

The
BATTLE
PLAN
for
PRAYER

BIBLE STUDY

STEPHEN KENDRICK
ALEX KENDRICK
WITH TRAVIS AGNEW

LifeWay Press®
Nashville, Tennessee

Published by LifeWay Press® © Copyright 2015 Kendrick Brothers, LLC. Used under license, all rights reserved.

Reprinted 2016

No part of this book may be reproduced or transmitted in any form or by any means, electronic or mechanical, including photocopying and recording, or by any information storage or retrieval system, except as may be expressly permitted in writing by the publisher. Requests for permission should be addressed in writing to LifeWay Press; One LifeWay Plaza; Nashville, TN 37234-0152.

ISBN: 9781430040453

Item: 005728499

Dewey Decimal Classification: 248.84

Subject Heading: PRAYER/SPIRITUAL WARFARE/SPIRITUAL LIFE

Unless otherwise noted, Scripture quotations are taken from the New American Standard Bible®, Copyright ©1960, 1962, 1963, 1968, 1971, 1972, 1973, 1975, 1977, 1995 by The Lockman Foundation. Used by permission. (www.lockman.org). Scripture marked HCSB taken from the Holman Christian Standard Bible®, copyright © 1999, 2000, 2002, 2003 by Holman Bible Publishers. Used by permission. Scripture marked NIV taken from THE HOLY BIBLE, NEW INTERNATIONAL VERSION®, NIV® Copyright © 1973, 1978, 1984, 2011 by Biblica, Inc.® Used by permission. All rights reserved worldwide. Scripture marked KJV is from the King James Version Bible. Scripture marked NKJV is from the New King James Version. Copyright © 1979, 1980, 1982, Thomas Nelson, Inc., Publishers.

Printed in the United States of America

To order additional copies of this resource, write to LifeWay Christian Resources Customer Service; One LifeWay Plaza; Nashville, TN 37234-0113; fax 615.251.5933; phone toll free 800.458.2772; email *orderentry@lifeway.com*; order only at *www.lifeway.com*; or visit the LifeWay Christian Store serving you.

Adult Ministry Publishing
LifeWay Christian Resources
One LifeWay Plaza
Nashville, TN 37234-0152

CONTENTS

ABOUT THE AUTHOR

Stephen Kendrick is a speaker, film producer, and author with a ministry passion for prayer and discipleship. He is a cowriter and producer of the movies *WAR ROOM, Courageous, Facing the Giants,* and *Fireproof* and cowriter of the New York Times bestsellers *The Resolution for Men* and *The Love Dare.* Stephen is an ordained minister and speaks at conferences and men's events. He attended seminary, received a communications degree from Kennesaw State University, and now serves on the board of the Fatherhood CoMission. Stephen and his wife, Jill, live in Albany, Georgia, with their six children, where they are active members of Sherwood Church.

Alex Kendrick is an award-winning author gifted at telling stories of hope and redemption. He is best known as an actor, writer, and director of the films *Fireproof, Courageous, Facing the Giants,* and *WAR ROOM* and coauthor of the New York Times bestselling books *The Love Dare, The Resolution for Men, Fireproof* (the novel), and *Courageous* (the novel). In 2002, Alex helped found Sherwood Pictures and partnered with his brother Stephen to launch Kendrick Brothers Productions. He is a graduate of Kennesaw State University and attended seminary before being ordained into ministry. Alex and his wife, Christina, live in Albany, Georgia, with their six children. They are active members of Sherwood Church.

Travis Agnew's life mission is to make disciples. Married to his high school sweetheart, Amanda, Travis is the father of two sons and one daughter. Currently Family & Worship Pastor at North Side Baptist Church in Greenwood, SC, he also serves as adjunct religion instructor at Lander University. Travis graduated from North Greenville University with a B.A. in Christian Studies and a Music minor. Earning an M.Div. and D.Min. from The Southern Baptist Theological Seminary, his doctoral focus was on equipping parents to evangelize and disciple their children.

INTRODUCTION

Knowing the dynamics of battle is key to success for any army. Those in command gather intelligence about the enemy, they create a plan of attack, and they prepare to respond appropriately to ensure victory. Wise leaders choose their battles and fight to win.

As believers it is time for us to get our battle plan ready. It is time for us to strategically prepare and fight for our homes and families. It is time for us, as the church, to stand up for truth. And prayer is a powerful weapon that is absolutely necessary to ensure our victory in this spiritual battle. So, welcome to *The Battle Plan for Prayer* Bible study. All you need in this journey is this Bible study book and the videos, if your group chooses to use them.

We believe in the power of prayer. We've seen it in God's Word. We've seen prayer work in the lives of others. And we've experienced it first hand in our own lives. It's undeniable to us that God willingly, readily, and powerfully answers prayer. Stories in the Bible may seem far-fetched until you experience God and answered prayer for yourself.

Many in our generation have lost sight of the power of prayer. We don't pray. Prayer is hard work. It's easier to go out and attempt to fix things ourselves than to pray. Because prayer requires us to be still, quiet, humble, dependent, and honest before a sovereign and holy God, prayer becomes our last resort. But prayer is so misunderstood and underutilized.

What would happen if churches really began to pray again? What if believers got right with the Lord and began to seek His face again? Second Chronicles 7:14 reminds us that if "My people who are called by My name humble themselves, pray and seek My face, and turn from their evil ways, then I will hear from heaven, forgive their sin, and heal their land."

We believe God is raising up an army of prayer warriors in our generation. We are asking you to go with us on this journey and equip yourself and others to pray more effectively. We will discuss types of prayer, hindrances to prayer, keys to effective prayer, praying strategically for the lost and for believers alike. We will be sharing real stories of answered prayer in our lives and in Christian history and we will be hearing from some of our generation's most respected prayer teachers and trainers and learning from them as well.

 We're also excited to introduce the War Room Prayer app. Keep your war room on your phone and manage prayer requests for easy access. Available for iOS and Android. This amazingly simple tool will help you in your goal of becoming more devoted to prayer.

SESSION 1
DEVOTED
TO PRAYER

Welcome to Week 1 of *The Battle Plan for Prayer*. We hope this Bible study changes your prayer life in many ways. We can't wait to hear how God works and answers prayers as you complete this study and learn to pray more strategically and specifically.

Let's take a moment to get to know one another before we watch this week's video.

What drew you to this study?

What do you hope to gain from this study of prayer?

What are the most common prayers you pray now?

Do you have a story—in your life or the life of someone you know—of answered prayer? Share with the group if you feel comfortable.

Through this study, you will learn to pray for those around you. You will learn how to use the powerful weapon of prayer to fight life's battles and to grow closer to Christ.

Take a moment to pray with your group. Pray that God will teach you through this study. Pray for the open hearts and minds of those in your group. Pray that God will unify you as a group and help you to be vulnerable with one another for the next eight weeks. Thank Him for the opportunity to study His Word together.

SESSION 1

VIDEO NOTES

_____

_____

_____

_____

_____

_____

_____

_____

_____

_____

_____

_____

_____

_____

_____

_____

_____

_____

_____

_____

_____

_____

_____

_____

_____

_____

_____

Video sessions are available for download
at _www.lifeway.com/BattlePlan_

After viewing the video, discuss the following questions with your group.

What were the most important points for you personally during this video session?

Do you know anyone who is a person of prayer? What makes you say that about them?

Do you think we've lost a passion for prayer? Why or why not?

In the video we mentioned that prayer is not so much a posture or practice; it is all about a relationship. How does that information make prayer easier or harder for you?

Why do you think we sometimes make prayer a "last ditch effort" in our spiritual lives?

Take a moment and list seven specific things you want to pray about during this study. Bring them to the Lord now and commit to pray for these needs and issues weekly as you go through this study.

1.

2.

3.

4.

5.

6.

7.

Close this time with your group in prayer asking God to teach you how to pray more effectively through this Bible study. As you dismiss your group, don't forget to assign the following five daily devotions to be completed between now and your next meeting together.

PRAYER 101

What does the word *prayer* stir up in you? Does it make you feel comforted and at peace, or does it make you feel nervous and guilty? Write out some of your feelings about prayer as we jump into this study together.

When we really stop to think about prayer, we should quickly realize what a privilege it is. God does not have to communicate with us and doesn't need for us to communicate with Him. But, He chooses to. That's the love of God—He chooses to involve us in His work. He wants to have a relationship with us. He wants to show Himself mighty in our lives and intercede on our behalf time and time again.

When you really stop to think about it, what amazes you about prayer?

The heart of prayer is simply talking to God. In this study, we are going to get a better grasp on this vital practice in our lives and then we are going to take it a step further to create a strategy for prayer. Through this study, you will learn to strategically pray for yourself, your spouse, your kids, your lost friends. But, we have to start with the basics and lay a foundation before we can build up to large prayer strategies.

So, back to the heart of prayer—how would you define *prayer*?

Some of the words that came up in your definition might have included: *petition, request, thanksgiving, praise*. If you feel so led, it would be great if you would share this definition with your group next time and hear what other people wrote down as well.

If God compiled a list of the top five prayers He hears, what do you think would make the list?

Most likely, the list you compiled revolved around individual crises or routine rituals. Those prayers are important, but God's Word instructs believers to be devoted to prayer. This means we must move beyond the status quo. As we're beginning this study, maybe you're hesitant to add one more thing to your already busy schedule.

What is your greatest struggle with prayer? Finding time to pray? Knowing what to pray? Something else?

Prayer isn't one more thing to add to your list. Prayer empowers the list. We are not asking you to add something new, but to do what you are already doing relying on God's power and provision instead. We are challenging you to devote yourself to prayer.

One of the game changers when it comes to prayer is recognizing how much God loves us and wants to hear from us. When we stop to remember how much God longs for us to walk so closely with Him, it really does change everything.

Take a moment to read Ephesians 3:16-18 (HCSB):

> *16 I pray that He may grant you, according to the riches of His glory, to be strengthened with power in the inner man through His Spirit, 17 and that the Messiah may dwell in your hearts through faith. I pray that you, being rooted and firmly established in love, 18 may be able to comprehend with all the saints what is the length and width, height and depth of God's love.*

Underline the words *pray* and *love* each time you see them.

How do you think your prayer life could be impacted if you prayed knowing that you are "rooted and firmly established in love"?

Prayer doesn't have to be something you are scared of or anxious about. If you remind yourself of your sure footing in the love of Christ, your prayers will hopefully come a little easier and be a little bolder. May God deepen your grasp of His love as you learn to boldly approach Him in a renewed devotion to prayer.

INSTRUCTIONS ON PRAYER

Right above 1 Timothy 2 in the HCSB, the heading "Instructions in Prayer" appears. So, let's read these instructions and unpack them today:

1 First of all, then, I urge that petitions, prayers, intercessions, and thanksgivings be made for everyone, 2 for kings and all those who are in authority, so that we may lead a tranquil and quiet life in all godliness and dignity. 3 This is good, and it pleases God our Savior, 4 who wants everyone to be saved and to come to the knowledge of the truth.

What other words are listed in verse 1 that mean *prayer*?

For whom specifically does Paul say we should pray?

The last verse here is what sets us in awe. Why does prayer please God?

Our God is a good God who longs for His people to come to salvation. We will talk more later in the study about praying specifically for those who are lost, but for now let's think a little bigger.

You came to this study with a hope to be better equipped for prayer. Maybe to pray more often, or to even begin to pray, or perhaps to pray with more intensity and focus. It is our hope that God will move you to a whole new level of prayer through your focus on it during this study, but since 1 Timothy tells us to pray for everyone, we would love for you to take some time to list out those specific people you want to be more strategic in praying for.

Make a list now and then beside each name write one main thing you want to pray over that person.

1.

2.

3.

4.

5.

6.

7.

8.

9.

10.

Now, if you haven't already done this, take a few minutes to do just that— pray about each person and the word you wrote for each person.

We would love for you to bookmark this page somehow so you can come back to this list over the next few weeks, not only to remember to keep praying for these people and the specific item for each person, but to also watch and see how God will work and move through those prayers.

DEVOTED
TO PRAYER

Paul commanded believers to be devoted to prayer (Rom. 12:12; Col. 4:2). While that sounds like a noble concept, what does that really mean? What does that type of devotion look like?

The Greek word for *devotion* Paul uses is *proskartereo* in these verses. The word is used ten times in the New Testament; five of them are associated with prayer and five are not. To help us understand this type of prayer devotion, let's look at how the verb is used each time.

> **In the verses below, the translation of *proskartereo* is in bold. Notice how it is used. Under each verse, make a note about what this teaches us concerning being devoted to prayer and discuss your observations the next time you meet as a group.**

• All these were **continually united** in prayer, along with the women, including Mary the mother of Jesus, and His brothers (Acts 1:14, HCSB).

• And they **devoted** themselves to the apostles' teaching, to the fellowship, to the breaking of bread, and to the prayers (Acts 2:42, HCSB).

• But we will **devote** ourselves to prayer and to the preaching ministry (Acts 6:4, HCSB).

• Rejoice in hope; be patient in affliction; be **persistent** in prayer (Rom. 12:12, HCSB).

• **Devote** yourselves to prayer; stay alert in it with thanksgiving (Col. 4:2, HCSB).

> **After studying the above verses, how would you describe what it means to be devoted to prayer?**

What have been the major prayer catalysts in your personal life? In other words, what things have caused you to become more devoted to prayer?

What would need to change in your life for you to be more devoted to prayer?

If it meant positively transforming your life and empowering your spiritual impact on others, would you be willing to make those changes?

In addition to the verses that used *proskartereo* ("devoted") concerning prayer, there are five other usages of the word in the New Testament. Studying these verses can actually help us get a better handle on how to become devoted to prayer.

In the verses below, the usage of *proskartereo* is in bold. Beside each verse, make notes of how this helps you better understand being "devoted" to prayer.

- Then He told His disciples to have a small boat **ready** for Him, so the crowd would not crush Him (Mark 3:9, HCSB).

- Then even Simon himself believed. And after he was baptized, he **went around constantly** with Philip and was astounded as he observed the signs and great miracles that were being performed (Acts 8:13).

- When the angel who spoke to him had gone, he called two of his household slaves and a devout soldier, who was one of those who **attended** him (Acts 10:7).

- And for this reason you pay taxes, since the authorities are God's public servants, **continually attending** to these tasks (Rom. 13:6, HCSB).

Out of these verses, what helps you most concerning being devoted to prayer?

Devotion involves committing to something consistently and frequently. To be consistently devoted to prayer, we have to train ourselves in this practice. It does not come naturally. We must train ourselves to be in constant communion with God.

Stop now to pray and ask God for help to repurpose your life as one who is devoted to prayer.

DAY 4

THE EXAMPLE
OF JESUS

When most people think of Jesus' prayer life, they default to the teaching we commonly refer to as the Lord's Prayer. While we will dive deep into this pivotal prayer template later in this study, Jesus' prayer ministry was not isolated to this famous teaching. In fact, His entire ministry was saturated in prayer.

Read the following passages that describe the prayer life of Jesus. Under each verse, make notes of what impacts you concerning His example.

- **[Early stages of ministry] - In the early morning, while it was still dark, Jesus got up, left the house, and went away to a secluded place, and was praying there (Mark 1:35).**

- **[Before making the selection of the twelve disciples] - It was at this time that He went off to the mountain to pray, and He spent the whole night in prayer to God (Luke 6:12).**

- **[After feeding the 5,000] - After He had sent the crowds away, He went up on the mountain by Himself to pray; and when it was evening, He was there alone (Matt. 14:23).**

- **[Before His crucifixion] - And He came out and proceeded as was His custom to the Mount of Olives; and the disciples also followed Him. When He arrived at the place, He said to them, "Pray that you may not enter into temptation." And He withdrew from them about a stone's throw, and He knelt down and began to pray (Luke 22:39-41).**

What are some of the aspects of Jesus' prayer life that impact you most?

At what times of day did Jesus pray?

In what kinds of situations did Jesus set aside time to pray?

Not only did Jesus teach on the importance of prayer, He modeled this devotion to prayer.

Have you ever wondered why Jesus needed to pray? If Jesus was God, why did He need to take time to pray?

Although Jesus was fully God while He was on earth, Scripture also teaches that He "kept increasing in wisdom and stature, and in favor with God and men" (Luke 2:52). Prayer was Jesus' communication to God the Father while He lived on earth. Prayer was His means, along with the Holy Spirit, of knowing and carrying out God's will. Prayer was a vital part of the intimate fellowship between God the Father and Christ His Son.

Think of the most important relationship in your life. How strong would that relationship be if the communication between you stopped today?

Based on Jesus' prayer life, what is the primary function of prayer?

If Jesus, the Son of God, was constantly dependent upon the Father through prayer, how could we possibly think it is not necessary for us?

As you close today, pray and ask God to show you some changes you need to make to become more consistent and dependent upon Him in prayer. (Hint: Being a part of this study is a huge step in the right direction. God will be faithful as you work to become devoted to prayer.)

PRAYER STRATEGY TARGET

It is our hope and prayer that you dive deep into the topic of prayer through this Bible Study. We have a feeling that you are hoping and praying the same thing. God will be faithful as you focus on this over these next eight weeks. It is also our prayer, though, that you leave at the end of this study with a firm grasp on how to pray for those around you—your friends, family members, the lost, those in authority over you, and more—in a strategic way.

To do that, we have developed a sort of road map—in the form of a Prayer Strategy Target.

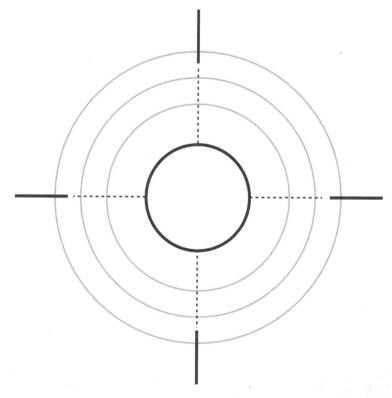

We will work through this target together over the coming weeks in each "Day 5" of our homework. By the end of the study you will know how to utilize this target and pray specifically and strategically for others.

We want to start today with the vertical and horizontal lines on the target. They represent the cross. Prayer begins with the cross of Jesus Christ.

The cross allows us access to the Father.

John 14:6 says:

> *Jesus said to him, "I am the way, and the truth, and the life; no one comes to the Father but through Me."*

Our relationship to God through Jesus is the key to healthy and effective prayers. We need to be vertically aligned with God through the cross before we can do anything else.

As Scripture says, "He saved us, not on the basis of deeds which we have done in righteousness, but according to His mercy, by the washing of regeneration and renewing by the Holy Spirit, whom He poured out upon us richly through Jesus Christ our Savior, so that being justified by His grace we would be made heirs according to the hope of eternal life" (Titus 3:5-7).

With this in mind, it is important to make sure we submit to God's plan and are saved God's way through Jesus, not on our own. Jesus said, "Truly, truly, I say to you, unless one is born again he cannot see the kingdom of God" (John 3:3). Salvation comes from the Lord, not man. It is a spiritual transformation God brings about within someone's heart and life. No individual or church can manufacture it. But God does it as we repent and trust Christ alone by faith.

We understand that in this Bible study setting we are speaking to all different kinds of people. Non-believers, seekers, new believers, seasoned Christians, wayward Christians —you name it. No matter where you are, though, take a moment and stop and evaluate your relationship with Jesus.

If you aren't certain of your relationship to God through Jesus, would you reach out to your small group leader or someone on your church staff to begin to talk this out with them? They will be honored to help you.

If you've repented and trusted Jesus Christ as your Lord and Savior, this is the foundation for a strong prayer life. If you are clear in your heart that you have salvation, would you consider praying and thanking God for this incredible gift? Also, ask God if there are specific areas of your relationship with Him that might need a tune up. Allow Him to work and write out any notes or prayers on that topic below.

Now do something that might not seem so obvious. Pray about your prayer life. Write out a description of the kind of prayer warrior you desire to become. Then pray over each aspect and ask God to make that a reality in you.

May God do a great and lasting work in your heart and draw you deeper and closer into a loving relationship with Him like never before!

SESSION 2

SCHEDULED AND SPONTANEOUS PRAYER

Each week, we'll review here what we learned in personal study the previous week. Refer back to your notes when answering these questions with the group if you'd like.

What new thing did you learn or what stood out to you about prayer this week?

What is your greatest struggle with prayer? Finding time to pray? Knowing what to pray? Something else? (Day 1)

How would you describe what it means to be devoted to prayer? (Day 3)

What would need to change in your life to become more devoted to prayer? (Day 3)

What are some of the things that impact you concerning the prayer life of Jesus? (Day 4)

Do you have any prayer requests from Day 2 that you would be comfortable sharing with the group so they can also be praying?

SESSION 2

VIDEO NOTES

After viewing the video, discuss the following questions with your group.

What were the most important points for you personally during this video session?

What are some practical ideas for praying without ceasing?

What do you think about writing down your prayers? Have you ever written out your prayers? How did that help you? Do you have any tips to share with the group?

Take time to talk about the different types of spontaneous prayer. Is there one that comes more natural to you? One that's more difficult for you?

What does "faith like a child" look like in prayer?

Do you ever feel uncomfortable in prayer? Discuss the difference between a holy discomfort in prayer and an unholy discomfort.

What is your biggest takeaway or challenge from this video that you want to try to put into practice this week? Finding more scheduled time to pray? Praying more in spontaneous ways? Writing your prayers down? Share that with the group and pray and ask God to help you make these things a reality this week.

Read Mark 1:35 and Nehemiah 1:3-6. What do these two passages communicate about when Jesus and Nehemiah prayed?

Pray together as a group about God making you devoted and effective in prayer. Using the requests you wrote on page 9, close by praying for one another. Remind each other to complete the five days of homework before your next meeting.

SCHEDULED PRAYER PART 1

In a study like this one, we can run the risk of getting excited about prayer without actually accomplishing it. Instead of merely getting energized about a battle plan for prayer, you need to ensure that you set yourself up for success.

As we continue this journey, take some practical steps to ensure you will be more persistent in prayer. Some prayer times are scheduled and some are spontaneous. We will look at scheduled today and tomorrow and the spontaneous prayer later this week.

Read Jesus' description of how He said we should pray in Matthew 6:5-8. Underline or circle key words and phrases.

5 When you pray, you are not to be like the hypocrites; for they love to stand and pray in the synagogues and on the street corners so that they may be seen by men. Truly I say to you, they have their reward in full. 6 But you, when you pray, go into your inner room, close your door and pray to your Father who is in secret, and your Father who sees what is done in secret will reward you. 7 And when you are praying, do not use meaningless repetition as the Gentiles do, for they suppose that they will be heard for their many words. 8 So do not be like them; for your Father knows what you need before you ask Him.

What are three things you discovered about prayer from this passage?

1.

2.

3.

What is Jesus condemning in these verses?

Jesus is not condemning the act of public prayer itself, but rather a wrong motive.

Who is the intended audience for our prayers?

Prayer is ultimately not about you, but about God. It is not about your glory or your will, but about His glory and His will. Jesus encourages true believers to take prayer into a private place because our prayers are not for stroking our ego, but for knowing and pleasing God alone.

Do you have a private room designated for prayer—a prayer closet or a special spot? Do you have a specific time you meet with God? Why or why not?

You may not have the physical space in your home to claim a separate room as a private prayer sanctuary, but you can make some adjustments to set yourself up for success when it comes to prayer. It's time to get practical.

How can you reclaim a space and a time in your home to pray regularly?

Hold yourself accountable. In the space below, write down a place and time that you will set aside for prayer for the remainder of this week.

Pray and commit this blueprint to God
and get to work on it today!

SCHEDULED PRAYER PART 2

In the video this week we mentioned some people in the Bible who had specific times that they prayed in a scheduled way. Let's look at some of those examples now and see what God might teach us.

DAVID - PSALM 55:16-17, NIV

16 As for me, I call to God,
and the Lord saves me.
17 Evening, morning and noon
I cry out in distress,
and he hears my voice.

When specifically did David pray according to this passage?

David's example is inspiring. It's an honor that we can look back thousands of years and read so many of his specific prayers in the Psalms. Not all of David's prayers were joyful prayers. In the verses shown, he is crying out in distress to God, but notice he does it in a strategic, scheduled way.

Later in the Psalms David talks again about scheduled prayer.
Read Psalm 119:164.

How many times does David say he prays in this passage?

Before we talk more about this, let's look quickly at Daniel.

DANIEL - DANIEL 6:10-11

10 Now when Daniel knew that the document was signed, he entered his house (now in his roof chamber he had windows open toward Jerusalem); and he continued kneeling on his knees three times a day, praying and giving thanks before his God, as he had been doing previously. 11 Then these men came by agreement and found Daniel making petition and supplication before his God.

What you can't tell just by reading these verses is that Daniel was in a time of extreme trouble during this season of his life. He knew that he could be arrested and killed for his faith. Even then, Daniel prayed and trusted. God answered his prayers and rescued him from the mouths of lions.

How many times on average would you estimate that you pray each day?

How many of those times are scheduled and how many are spontaneous?

You may not be able to start to have seven times of scheduled prayer a day, or even three. But, we challenge you to at least start with one time. If you desire to add more, then great, but at least start with one scheduled time and see if you can keep it up throughout the course of this study. We are confident that as you devote scheduled time to prayer, you are going to see it impact your life.

Write down a specific time you plan to pray this week. Jot a reminder on a sticky note or set an alarm on your phone as a way to remember the time you've committed to scheduled prayer.

We will talk more about spontaneous prayers over the next few days, as both spontaneous and scheduled prayers are important in a believer's life.

SPONTANEOUS PRAYER PART 1

It is extremely helpful to have a scheduled time and a sacred space in which you pray. Scripture teaches us to pray continually. Unexpected obstacles will charge at you this week and you need to be prepared for those spontaneous times of prayer.

Read 1 Thessalonians 5:17 and write it out in the space below.

Depending on the translation of Scripture you use, the word used in this verse might be *constantly, regularly, continually,* or *without ceasing.*

Do you believe that this instruction is actually possible? Why or why not?

What would it look like for this verse to be practically applied in your life this week?

On a corporate level, churches can "pray without ceasing" by taking turns and praying in shifts throughout the day. On an individual level, we can make prayer a natural and regular part of our day.

As you think through your schedule over the next 24 hours, you'll realize there are probably some times where you are going to need to go to God in prayer and your prayer closet will not be accessible.

In the next 24 hours, when would be pivotal times when you could pause and pray?

Identifying pivotal times to pray is important and one of the first steps in becoming more devoted to prayer. But we can't always predict when we will need to take time to pray. In order to truly put 1 Thessalonians 5:17 into practice we must remain in close fellowship with God and be aware of His presence in our lives. The ultimate goal of course is for prayer to be a regular and frequent habit throughout your day.

Come up with some practical reminders. You could include hanging notes in strategic places, setting reminders on your phone, or teaming up with a friend to hold each other accountable. Write down at least three tangible reminders you can use to increase your prayer frequency over the next 24 hours. Now, commit it to God in prayer.

Today we will finish our time together discussing different times of spontaneous prayers. The more you get in the habit of bringing conversation with God into a daily rhythm in your life, the more you can sense and feel God's presence and guidance day in and day out.

NEWNESS

Any time there is something new in your life, it is worth spending some time praying about it and dedicating it to God.

What is something new in your life you can pray for now? Some ideas could be: a new house, new car, new friend, a new believer who may have just found Jesus, or even simply a new day or new season of life.

Write down two new things in your life right now and pray for them.

NEEDS

From day to day we will have different needs arise in our life. God knows what these needs are and longs to come to you and meet you in those needs. Maybe you have a financial need, an emotional need, or a physical need.

Write down two needs and spend a moment praying about them.

SPONTANEOUS PRAYER PART 2

Today we will finish our discussion about specific reminders for spontaneous prayers. Remember, when conversation with God becomes a part of your daily rhythm, you will be able to sense His presence and guidance even more. Let's finish looking at occasions that should prompt us towards spontaneous prayer.

CONFUSION

Isaiah 55:9 says that God's thoughts are higher than our thoughts. We often can't see the big picture, so it is understandable to have times of confusion, wondering why something isn't working out like we thought it would.

What is something that is confusing in your life right now that you might want to ask God to help you see more clearly? Write that down and pray about it now.

CRISIS

Perhaps you are in a time of crisis right now. If not, I am guessing you can think of someone who is in a crisis and could use your prayers. In our social media-driven world, people post about the struggles they are having online all the time. Just take a look at one of your social media feeds, and when you see or notice someone in a crisis—stop and pray.

Write any situation that God brings to your mind in this category and take a moment to lift it back up to Him in prayer.

SIN

Nothing blocks your prayer life like sin you refuse to confess and surrender to God. We need to pray for forgiveness and repent in order to re-establish healthy communion with the Father. So often our initial reaction to sin is to cover it up, dismiss it, and try to forget about it and move on. We should never put petty sin above our loving God. If you get in the habit of confessing your sin to God you will find yourself coming to Him more often for all areas in your life because you are freed up from the weight of that sin.

Write down the names or initials of specific sins you need to confess, if you feel comfortable doing that here, and pray that God would forgive you and heal your heart in that area. Ask Him to help you find your satisfaction in Him instead.

STRESS

We know that even now something is tugging on your mind, maybe something that you have to do, or perhaps a relationship that is challenging. It is hard to get away from the everyday stresses of life. Because they are such a daily issue in our lives, though, we should get in the habit of pausing and bringing those stresses to our Father.

Take a moment and write down the top three things you are stressed about at this time and remind God of your need for Him during those stressful moments.

BLESSINGS

Now for a positive turn. God is always good and He longs to give good gifts to His children (Matt. 7:11). Even during dark times in our lives, we can list off multiple blessings that God has given to us. Joy follows gratefulness.

Take some time to write some of those down and thank God that He is good.

BURDENS

Come to Me, all of you who are weary and burdened, and I will give you rest.

MATTHEW 11:28, HCSB

God wants us to bring Him our burdens. Let's take Him up on that now and anytime we feel burdened for the lost, our culture, or those in desperate need.

Note some of the burdens that come to mind here and bring those to the Lord.

REQUESTS

This is often the spontaneous part of prayer that comes easy. When others request prayer, we should lift them up. God also wants us to bring our requests to Him but to do so with the right motives. James 4:3 is clear on that:

You ask and do not receive, because you ask with wrong motives, so that you may spend it on your pleasures.

A good exercise to do as you bring your requests to God is to do a gut check to be sure your motives are in the right place. We should never let lust, greed, or pride motivate our prayers.

Take a moment to bring your requests before God.

REJOICING

Philippians 4:4 says, "Rejoice in the Lord always." We have so much to rejoice over, even in hard times. Successes, accomplishments, answered prayers, and celebrations should prompt prayers of praise and thanksgiving back to God.

Spend a moment writing reasons to rejoice and celebrating something good in prayer.

PRAYER STRATEGY TARGET

As promised, in each Day 5 we are going to spend some time working through our Prayer Strategy Target. Here is a reminder of what it looks like:

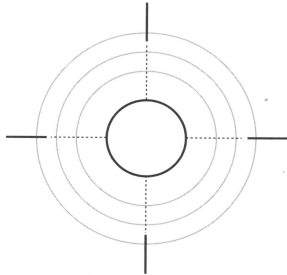

Last week we evaluated our vertical relationship with God and were reminded of how prayer is made possible through Jesus' death on the cross.

This week we want to look at the horizontal line across the middle of the target. It represents being aligned well with others in order for prayer to be most effective. God wants us to walk in love and in unity with others. Bitterness toward others can hinder our prayer lives. Also, if we have wronged others and not made it right, God wants us to stop delaying and to make things right.

We will hit on this topic in more depth throughout our time together over the next few weeks but let's pause and evaluate where we are on that horizontal line just for a moment together.

An interesting passage in Genesis 11 describes the construction of the tower of Babel. In this biblical account, ungodly people decided to build a city with an enormous tower for their own glory and prestige. They planned it out and began the challenge, and at first found success in their efforts. But God looked down from heaven and basically said, "Because of their unity, nothing will be impossible for them" (see v. 6). So He intervened. He divided them by changing their communication into numerous languages to prevent them from finishing their prideful monument. In the confusion and chaos, they abandoned the project and separated themselves by language, spreading out across the land.

What is so striking about this passage of Scripture is that God Himself noted that when people are unified, they are able to exert tremendous power and momentum. Even ungodly people! So imagine how powerful unity can be for people who worship and obey the God of the universe. If they seek the Lord and act in unity, nothing can stop them.

That's why the Enemy does everything possible to keep God's people divided. Because once we come together in unity, we gain momentum and take ground for the kingdom. United prayer is powerful. But prayer from a divided people … well, not so much. This is why removing bitterness toward others and choosing to forgive is so crucial. In fact, any pride or selfishness should be seen as an enemy of unified prayer.

In John 17, Jesus prayed a beautiful prayer, asking God to unify believers into one body, that the world would know He was sent by God to bring salvation to the world (v. 21). Psalm 133:1 echoes the same theme: "Behold, how good and how pleasant it is for brothers to dwell together in unity!"

God loves and blesses unity. It speaks volumes about the body of Christ when we worship together and love one another as God intended. It also draws attention to our Savior, who died to cleanse our sins and now lives to intercede for us to God the Father. When people see unity, they see purpose, love, and power. It's attractive and beautiful. And when an army of people work together to accomplish a goal, they become a formidable force indeed.

JOHN 13:34-35 SAYS:

34 A new commandment I give to you, that you love one another, even as I have loved you, that you also love one another. 35 By this all men will know that you are My disciples, if you have love for one another.

Jesus' words here are clear and the model Jesus gave us through His life and ministry makes it even more clear—we are to love our neighbor. And our neighbor is anyone and everyone who is a part of our lives.

So, before we can tackle this concept of prayer in a serious way, we need to not only evaluate our relationship with God, but also our relationship with others.

We will talk about this concept more in detail in the coming weeks, but for now, take a moment and consider any strained or broken relationships that you have in your life. Do not only bring them to the Lord in prayer, but ask Him what you need to do in order to make some of these relationships right again.

Relationships are complicated, we know, but the Bible says:

If possible, so far as it depends on you, be at peace with all men.
ROMANS 12:18

Take a moment and talk to the Lord about any relationships that come to mind that need to be made right. For the sake of Christ and for the sake of gaining a more powerful prayer life, make a point to do something toward reconciliation this week. Pray about it now.

SESSION 3

TYPES OF PRAYER

Welcome back! Take a few moments and answer some of these questions together as you recap this past week's homework.

What stood out to you about praying scheduled and spontaneous prayers?

Are you more likely to pray scheduled prayers or spontaneous? Why?

Do you have a private room designated for prayer—a prayer closet or a special spot? Do you have a specific time you meet with God? Why or why not? (Day 1)

How can our group help hold you accountable to have scheduled times of prayer? (Day 1)

What would it look like for you to "pray continually"? (Day 3)

What did you learn about how our relationships impact our prayer life? (Day 5)

SESSION 3

VIDEO NOTES

_____

_____

_____

_____

_____

_____

_____

_____

_____

_____

_____

_____

_____

_____

_____

_____

_____

_____

_____

_____

_____

_____

_____

_____

_____

_____

Video sessions are available for download
at *www.lifeway.com/BattlePlan*

Watch the video with your group and discuss the following questions.

What were the most important points for you personally during this video session?

What types of adoration were familiar to you? What types were new? What did you learn about adoration?

Discuss this phrase, "Prayer without repentance never reaps the transformation of culture the way prayer with repentance does." What do you think that means? What does prayer without repentance look like? What does prayer with repentance look like?

Discuss the three things mentioned that we can add to our list of thanksgiving.

What are some practical steps you can take to express thanksgiving when you are tempted to speak unwholesome talk?

What are some of the reasons God says "wait"? Have you ever had to wait? What did you learn from that time?

Of the four types of prayer mentioned (Adoration, Confession, Thanksgiving, and Supplication), which ones do you tend toward and which one do you most neglect?

How might starting your prayers with adoration, confession, and thanksgiving better prepare you for supplication prayers?

Pray together as a group for one another. Ask God to help you to become more balanced and effective in every type of prayer.

YOUR NAME
BE HOLY

Our Father in heaven, Your name be honored as holy. Your kingdom come, Your will be done on earth as it is in heaven.
MATTHEW 6:9-10, HCSB

This week, we are going to unpack the Lord's Prayer by focusing on the individual petitions that Jesus taught us to make. The first petition is a desire for the name of God to be honored as holy. His name should be set apart as greater and more special than all other names. His name—like His attributes—is like none other. Calling upon the name of the Lord is like dialing His specific phone number. It initiates direct communication with God Almighty.

Read Exodus 20:7. What are ways that people misuse the name of the Lord?

Why is this significant enough for God to address the issue as one of the Ten Commandments?

Read Philippians 2:10-11. Scripture teaches that not everyone will follow Jesus and go to heaven (Matt. 25:31-46), so what do you think it means that every knee will bow at Jesus' name and every tongue confess that He is Lord?

Read Psalm 135:13. How is God's reputation related to His name?

We must remember that prayer is not based upon our name, but God's name. God's name alone is holy, reigning, supreme. It is perfect, and more powerful than any name. More honored. Higher than every other name. It invites God's presence. It rebukes evil. It saves us. It is to be worshiped. That's why we must never take any of God's names in vain or use them flippantly. Rather, we praise and worship His name while honoring His attributes, power, and authority.

The next petition in the model prayer asks for God's kingdom and will to advance on the earth. Again, prayer is not about our plans and our kingdom, but His. When we pray, we are not seeking to bend God to our ever-changing, imperfect desires. We are yielding our lives to His perfect and eternal will. May His kingdom come and His will be done.

Thankfully the Bible talks a good deal about God's will. Look up the verses below and write down beside each verse what God's will is, according to the passage.

Micah 6:8

1 Thessalonians 4:3

1 Thessalonians 5:18

1 Timothy 2:3-4

As we pray, God amazingly reveals His will and ways to us, and then starts to align our hearts and minds with His. We yield to His perfect and powerful lordship. Christ is the "head of the body, the church," worthy of being ascribed "first place in everything" (Col. 1:18). As Jesus prayed, "not My will, but Yours be done …" (Luke 22:42), we too should pray, "Your kingdom come and Your will be done … in me and in my life." We follow where He lovingly leads.

In your time of prayer today, focus on the name of God. Pray that His name would be trusted and always honored in your life. Also, submit to God by faith and ask His kingdom to come and His will to be done in your life right now and in today's circumstances. Then, expect great things to happen as a result.

OUR DAILY BREAD

Give us this day our daily bread.
MATTHEW 6:11

This petition is asking God to provide for our needs. After their Exodus from Egypt, the nation of Israel wandered through the wilderness and complained of their lack of food and water. God promised to "rain bread from heaven" (Ex. 16:4) for the people. One interesting fact about this bread was its unique nature of being a daily provision.

Then the Lord said to Moses, "Behold, I will rain bread from heaven for you; and the people shall go out and gather a day's portion every day, that I may test them, whether or not they will walk in My instruction.
EXODUS 16:4

Why did God want the people to gather just enough for that day rather than stockpiling the food?

11 And the Lord spoke to Moses, saying, 12 "I have heard the grumblings of the sons of Israel; speak to them, saying, 'At twilight you shall eat meat, and in the morning you shall be filled with bread; and you shall know that I am the Lord your God.'
EXODUS 16:11-12

How did God's provision correspond with the people's understanding of Him?

Just like He promised, God provided for the people. When the people saw the "fine flakes" of bread on the ground, "they asked one another, 'What is it?' because they didn't know what it was" (Ex. 16:14-15, HCSB). The word *manna* literally means, *what is it.*

These former slaves had become dependent upon the provision of their taskmasters. Now free from their control and their provision, they were without access to basic needs. In this dependent and helpless state, God provided for them. It was a test to trust Him daily for what they needed. There was no planning for the future. They had to trust God one day at a time.

Think about a time when you were completely dependent on someone else. Did you learn to trust the person on whom you were dependent? Why or why not?

Hopefully, you see the connection between the Exodus narrative and Jesus' prayer. "Our Father, will you give us our daily bread?" We are not worrying about tomorrow's bread. We are asking for today's physical and spiritual needs and nourishment to be provided by God. We are focusing on the real needs at hand—one day at a time.

In utter dependence, it is this acknowledgment: God, if you don't feed us, we won't eat.

What do you genuinely need right now? Have you prayed about it?

What are the genuine needs of your church? Have you prayed about them?

Instead of doing what you can do to fix these situations, have you asked God to show Himself again as the Lord who provides (Gen. 22:14)?

Start praying specifically today for God's gracious provision in each of these situations. Jesus promised, "Ask and it will be given to you" (Matt. 7:7).

FORGIVE US OUR DEBTS

*And forgive us our debts, as we also
have forgiven our debtors.*
MATTHEW 6:12

This petition is unique compared to the others. This request for pardon comes with a distinct stipulation: forgive us as we have forgiven others.

We understand that we need forgiveness. None of us are righteous; all have sinned against God (Rom. 3:23). And we know that the wages of sin is death (Rom. 6:23). Therefore, we are in need of a judicial forgiveness from God—a once for all pardon that allows us to receive salvation. Once we have that type of forgiveness, we are justified before God, at peace with God, and have righteousness from God through faith in Christ. Our salvation is as secure as the eternally powerful hands that hold it (John 10:27-19).

When Jesus died upon the cross, how many of your sins had not been committed yet?

Why, then, do you believe we ask God to forgive our sins regularly if He has already forgiven them once and for all?

We ask regularly for forgiveness because in addition to needing judicial forgiveness we also need a relational forgiveness. For example, when spouses disagree, it does not change the status of their relationship but it does change the fellowship within the relationship. If you have received the gospel and God has made you a new creation (2 Cor. 5:17), the status of your relationship with God does not change. You don't need to get saved and be justified again every time you sin. But you are in need of relational forgiveness and must walk in the light and in honest confession before God if you want to stay in close fellowship with Him (1 John 1:5-10).

The penitent heart you present before God acknowledges you have sinned and you are sorry about what you have done (Ps. 51:3-4). But a truly repentant heart will turn from the sin of "unforgiveness" and extend forgiveness to others as well.

With that frame of understanding, answer these questions:

Do I really want to pray that God would show me the kind of grace I have shown others?

What words would you use to describe the manner in which you have forgiven others?

Oftentimes, we may reword our "unforgiveness" like this:

- "Well, I can forgive but I refuse to forget."

- "I forgive them but I never want to be around them."

- "I'll forgive them only after they suffer a while and get what's coming to them."

Read Psalm 103:8-13. What do these verses tell us about how God forgives?

Jesus' forgiveness is once and for all. When we are forgiven of our sins, we are a new creation. God does not dwell on our old selves—our sin—but looks at us through the righteousness of Christ.

Is there anyone you need to forgive? Someone who wronged you but you keep holding anger in your heart against them? The name probably just popped into your mind even as you try to remove it quickly.

Pray today that you may be able to extend a heart of forgiveness for that person. Ask God to help you always willingly forgive others in the same manner He willingly forgives you.

DO NOT BRING US INTO TEMPTATION

*And do not bring us into temptation,
but deliver us from the evil one.*
MATTHEW 6:13, HCSB

These final two petitions pray for protection from temptation and the Evil One. It is a cry for help to keep us away from things that would damage our integrity.

Don't miss the power of the plural pronouns here. What Jesus prayed is important but what He didn't pray is also important. He didn't pray: "Do not bring *Me* into temptation, but deliver *Me* from the evil one." This kind of individualistic, independent mindset was not part of His prayer. If one person commits sin, the entire group deals with the consequences. Regardless of what we think, our decisions affect others greatly.

Stop for a minute and really think about the gravity of your decisions.

If you fall into temptation, how would that impact your family?

If you are not being like Christ, how does that impact your community?

If you are not walking closely with God, how does that impact your church?

My sin affects us. Your sin affects us. None of us is an island. We are the church, and we are the body of Christ. When the foot suffers, the entire body staggers (1 Cor. 12:26).

Read Matthew 6:13 again. When Jesus prayed that God would not bring us into temptation, this statement does not mean that God normally employs such methods. We know that God is not tempted by evil "and He Himself does not tempt anyone" (Jas. 1:13). God has also promised that every time we are tempted He provides a way of escape (1 Cor. 10:13). Jesus is able to come to our aid since He was tempted just like us yet He never sinned.

Instead, of asking God to remove all temptation, our prayer should be more like this: "God, keep me on Your righteous path. Sound the alarm when temptation is near. Keep my eyes open and my heart alert. Remind me that I could fall into the very sin that I hate. Cause me to hate and acknowledge any sin that so easily ensnares me. Awaken me to the reality of an Enemy who prowls around like a roaring lion seeking to devour" (1 Pet. 5:8).

At this point, let's get specific. If you feel uncomfortable writing down details in this book, feel free to shorthand it or code it somehow, but really get honest with this question:

If the Evil One wanted to take me out, what strategy would he likely use? What temptation would he employ? In what areas have I been pridefully letting my guard down?

By the way, if you don't have an answer for this question, you may be in a dangerous blind spot and closer to spiritual ruin than you think. Take this opportunity to pray more defensively so that you will not be taken advantage of by Satan's schemes (2 Cor. 2:11).

If these temptations come in certain environments which you can avoid, talk with God and make a battle plan. Get specific. What temptations do you need help avoiding? What strategies of the Enemy do you need to realize? Pray through these areas and ask God for deliverance from our evil adversary.

PRAYER STRATEGY TARGET

As is our typical Day 5 practice, we are coming back together to discuss the Prayer Strategy Target. We promise we will start to let you write in the target, but this week we need to discuss one more foundational piece.

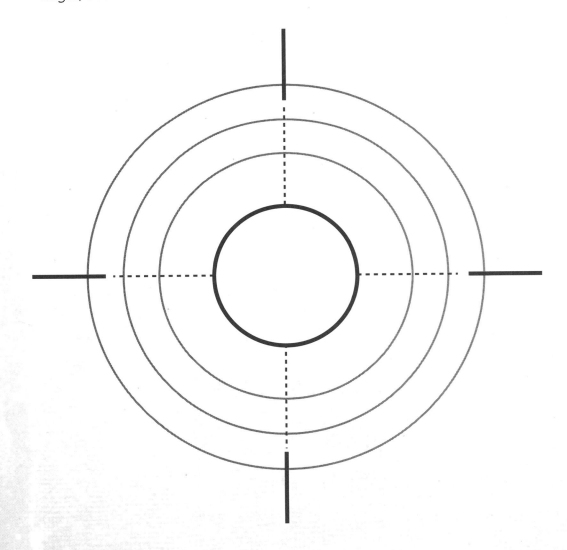

The circle in the middle will be where you eventually write the names of the people you are praying for, but today we want to talk about that circle itself. On the chart the circle in the middle represents the heart of the person praying. The condition of your heart affects your prayers.

Consider the following verses:

The prayer of a righteous person is powerful and effective.
JAMES 5:16, NIV

If I regard wickedness in my heart, the Lord will not hear.
PSALM 66:18

No one is saying you have to be perfect, but what these verses are saying is that the condition of your heart does matter when you pray.

James said the reason for a delay in God's answer is not always simply a timing issue. Sometimes "you ask and do not receive, because you ask with wrong motives, so that you may spend it on your pleasures" (Jas. 4:3). If lust, greed, bitterness, or pride is at the heart of a request, God may veto an answer in order to guard us from the hurt or idolatry that could result from the toxic request.

The first chapter of Proverbs says, "They will call on me, but I will not answer; they will seek me diligently but they will not find me, because they hated knowledge and did not choose the fear of the LORD" (vv. 28–29). Their attitude and behavior—the true condition of their hearts—stood between their request for help and its arrival. If they were ready to listen, however, if they would get their hearts right, their plight would be much better.

What are some areas of your heart where you feel the Lord is convicting you right now? And what are some ways you need to talk with Him about those things?

Read and pray Psalm 139:23-24. Spend some time here making any notes and praying about the motives of your heart and get that right with God.

LOCKS AND KEYS OF PRAYER

In this week's personal study, you looked at the Lord's Prayer as an example of the kinds of prayers we are called to pray. Discuss the following questions from the personal study with your group.

What did you learn about treating God's name as holy?

Share with the group about a time when you were completely dependent on someone else. How did that feel? Did you learn to trust the person on whom you were dependent? Why or why not? (Day 2)

Do you find it difficult or easy to forgive those who have hurt you? What in Day 3 changed your perspective of forgiveness?

What stood out to you in Day 4 about temptation?

How might your life be different in the future if you were to start daily engaging God for help and deliverance from evil instead of falling into it?

SESSION 4

VIDEO NOTES

_____
_____
_____
_____
_____
_____
_____
_____
_____
_____
_____
_____
_____
_____
_____
_____
_____
_____
_____
_____
_____
_____
_____
_____
_____

Video sessions are available for download
at _www.lifeway.com/BattlePlan_

Watch the Session 4 video and discuss the following as a group.

What were the most important points for you personally during this video session?

What is the significance of being right with God and others when praying?

Discuss the importance and difficulty of truly coming to God with clean hands and a pure heart.

"I don't have trouble hearing from God. What bothers me is what I hear." Does that resonate with you? How so?

You've probably heard people pray "in Jesus' name" many times. What stood out to you about that phrase in the video?

Discuss the locks that hinder prayer. Which ones concern or influence you most?

Discuss the keys of prayer. Which is hardest for you? What is easiest?

Why do you think God's Word specifically tells us what hinders or helps our prayer lives? What does that say about the heart of God and the importance of prayer?

Read James 5:16 and 1 Peter 3:8-12. Compare these two passages. What do they both communicate? How are they good summaries of the locks and keys of prayer?

Pray together that God helps you each to get right with Him and with one another and to get your heart right so that your prayers can become more powerful and effective.

LOCKS PART 1

Today and tomorrow, we are going to look at some biblical passages that tell us why God might not be answering our prayers. They will serve as warnings to us, no matter what phase of life we are in.

LOCK 1: UNCONFESSED SIN

Read Isaiah 59:1-2 and fill out the chart below.

What Hinders Prayer	Why Is This Important

Israel had questioned why the Lord had not heard their cries to Him (Isa. 58:3). In the verses above, Isaiah assured the nation of Israel that the reason their prayers were not answered was not because God is not powerful enough or even because He does not hear. It was because of their unconfessed sin. The people were not only sinful, they were unrepentant, resulting in a barrier between them and God.

What about you? Is there anything you need to go confess to the Lord today? Take a moment to do that right now.

Read Psalm 66:18-19 and fill out the chart below.

What Hinders Prayer	Why Is This Important

What is the difference between having malice in your heart and being aware of having malice in your heart?

Depending on your translation, the word in verse 18 may be *malice, iniquity, wickedness,* or something else. *Malice* is the desire to see harm, suffering, or evil come upon someone else. You might attempt to soften feelings of resentment toward someone by saying you don't want evil to come upon them but you simply don't want to see good come either. In reality, true love wants the best for others. Not desiring good is essentially desiring evil for him or her. The absence of good is evil. Jesus said we should love our enemies (Matt. 5:44).

When you become aware of malice in your heart, what is the appropriate response?

God may not be addressing your prayers because you are not addressing your sin. Ask God to make you aware of any other sin in your heart and confess that to Him. Make this prayer a regular habit. Identify and rectify. Keep communication lines open with God. Stay clean and close.

LOCK 2: FAMILY DISHARMONY

Another block to prayer is family disharmony. God takes seriously how we interact with those in our family. Children are called to honor parents. Fathers are instructed not to provoke their children but to bring them up in the instruction of the Lord in a gentle way. Husbands are called to love their wives, and wives are called to respect and support the leadership of their husbands.

The apostle Peter warns husbands that the way they treat their wives correlates with the effectiveness of their prayers.

Read 1 Peter 3:7 and fill out the chart below.

What Hinders Prayer	Why Is This Important

What does this verse mean? It means that a husband loves his wife and seeks to understand her. It means he cares for her and loves her the way Christ loves us. He protects her—when the world is falling apart, he is unwavering in his faith in God. He honors her. He doesn't insult, degrade, or intimidate her.

Men, don't bully any daughter of God under the guise of your masculinity. God doesn't appreciate handling his daughters in that manner. This is such an important issue, God's Word says that if a husband can't live with his wife in an understanding and honoring way, his prayers are hindered. His spiritual life has the parking brake on.

While this verse singles out husbands, that does not provide a free pass for everyone else. Wives, it is a good idea to live with your husbands in an understanding way, too.

Parents, what does it look like to live with your children in an understanding way? How might this attitude change your most important relationships?

Is there anyone in your family whom you have failed to treat with love and compassion? How so?

What changes do you need to make today to better honor your closest relationships so that your prayers are not hindered?

Ask God for forgiveness and talk with God about a reconciliation plan. Write down at least two or three ways you hope to see God work in that relationship. Commit your hopes to prayer. He is listening.

DAY 2

LOCKS PART 2

LOCK 3: BABBLING WORDS

One of the reasons people are intimidated to pray in public is due to a misunderstanding of prayer rhetoric. While we claim to believe that all prayers are equal, we tend to establish an hierarchy of prayers based on the level of impressive spiritual vocabulary used.

For many people, praying causes us to speak differently than how we speak at any other time. It causes us to repeat trite phrases, offer generic statements, and appear loftier than what we may actually be.

Jesus warned against practicing our righteousness before men to be noticed by them (Matt. 6:1). If we parade our prayers in a way to gain man's approval, we might momentarily impress people, but we will not also receive God's approval or the answer to our prayers.

Read warning Jesus provides in Matthew 6:7-8 and fill out the chart below.

What Hinders Prayer	Why Is This Important

Let's make an important distinction. The religious elite in Jesus' day repeated special words or phrases in their prayers to get God's and others' attention. The words themselves had no real meaning. Jesus cautioned against this practice not because of the repetition of the prayers, but because the prayers were not authentic. Jesus makes it clear in Matthew 6:8 that prayer is a matter of the heart more so than a matter of words.

What promise does Jesus offer concerning the Father and prayer in Matthew 6:8? How will knowing this affect your prayer life?

LOCK 4: FAITHLESS REQUESTS

Another reason God does not answer our prayers is because we offer faithless requests. Sure, we might pray to Him but we are often simultaneously doubting His goodness, concern, or ability to meet our needs.

Be honest about your attitude toward prayer. Do you trust or doubt God when you pray?

Even the disciples, who walked with Jesus daily, did not fully grasp the power of prayer.

Read Mark 9:17-29 and note the word *believe* each time it occurs. In this passage, a father asked Jesus' disciples to drive out a demon from his son, but they could not (v. 18).

What was Jesus' response when He learned of the disciples' failure (v. 19)?

See the father's honesty about his belief in Mark 9:24:

Immediately the boy's father cried out and said, "I do believe; help my unbelief."

When the disciples asked Jesus why they were unable to cast out the demon, He answered that this demon would not come out "by anything but prayer" (v. 29).

Prayer should always be our first line of defense.

Read James 1:6-8 and fill out the chart below.

What Hinders Prayer	Why Is This Important

Is prayer your first hope or your last-ditch effort?

Take time to confess your skepticism and your doubts. Be honest about your level of faith in God's abilities and ask Him to help your unbelief. Ask God to provide a more accurate understanding of who He is and what He can do. Then pray in faith knowing that "all things are possible to him who believes" (Mark 9:23).

LOCK 5: REQUESTS CONTRARY TO GOD'S WILL

One additional block to our prayers is when we ask for things that go against God's will.

Read 1 John 5:14-15 and fill out the chart to determine the importance of this warning.

What Hinders Prayer	Why Is This Important

Why do we desire to know God's will?

Make no mistake about it—God's purpose will prevail (Prov. 19:21). We just have to learn how to pray according to His will. How do you understand what the will of God is (Eph. 5:17)?

Read Romans 12:1-2.

God's Word reveals God's will. As we present ourselves to God, turn away from the backward values and vain thinking of the world and allow Him to renew our minds, God's heart, desires, and good and perfect will become vividly clear to us. Then when we pray according to God's will, our prayers will become amazingly powerful and effective.

In our study this week, we have investigated to see if we are allowing things in our lives that might hinder our prayers. Though we all can "stumble in many ways" (Jas. 3:2), we must take our relationship with a holy God seriously and deal with any issue that could hurt us spiritually. Knowing and loving God intimately is worth any sacrifice we need to make.

Take time to pray now. Confess any areas in your life that may be hindering your prayers and ask God to help you pursue His heart and overcome every one of these issues.

KEYS PART 1

KEY 1: STAY CONSISTENT
Read Philippians 4:8-9 and answer the questions below.

Why is it helpful to dwell on excellent things when anxiety and worry tend to grab your attention?

What are some excellent things you need to make a habit of dwelling upon?

In Philippians 4:7, Paul promised that the peace of God would guard the hearts of believers. In verses 8 and 9, Paul assured the Philippians that the God of peace would be with them. The peace of God only comes through the God of peace and His presence in our lives.

Are you aware of the peace of God and His presence in your life today?

Prayer is a powerful weapon against worry and anxious thoughts. By thanking God for His faithfulness in the past and turning every concern over to Him in prayer, He promises to guard our hearts and minds with His peace. Prayerfulness produces peacefulness. Without prayer, we will cloud our minds with useless worrying.

In the space below, get honest about those things causing you to be anxious. Fill out the columns to help get a perspective on your situation.

Concern	Is It Anxious-Worthy? (Phil. 4:6)	How to Pray	Verses to Pray

When we believe God is able to handle any and all of our concerns, there is no place left for worry. Be encouraged by Paul's final words to the Philippians:

19 And my God will supply all your needs according to His riches in glory in Christ Jesus. 20 Now to our God and Father be the glory forever and ever. Amen.
PHILIPPIANS 4:19-20

Pray individually over each concern you wrote above. Thank God in advance that He supplies all your needs. Pray for God's peace to replace your worry and guard your heart and mind.

KEY 2: TRUST GOD'S CHARACTER

Anxiousness can be a practical sign of a theological problem. When we become anxious, we are refusing to acknowledge who God is and what God can do.

In the Sermon on the Mount, Jesus addressed how to deal with anxiety. His solution is not in the collection of more desires met. His solution is in confidence shown in God's faithfulness and loving care. Our peace does not come from what we have but in the One who has us.

Read Jesus' description of the cure for anxiety in Matthew 6:25-34.

Jesus described different things that can cause us to become anxious. Out of the things mentioned, what can cause the greatest anxiety within you?

How has God provided for you in the last year? Get specific.

When we trace God's hand in our lives, it helps us understand that we are not on our own. He is near and He is actively involved in our lives.

What does it mean to seek God's kingdom?

What does it mean to seek God's righteousness?

How does seeking these two things help us remove anxiety from our lives?

We do not seek God in order to acquire more stuff from Him. We seek Him in order to experience more of Him. When we seek Him and His righteousness, our focus shifts from the earthly realm to the heavenly, from possessions to His presence.

Every kingdom has a ruler. Seeking God's kingdom and having faith that He is in control and has authority over your life is a surefire way to eliminate worry.

In your time of prayer today, thank God for His provision in your life. Be honest about any needs that you have today. Don't just pray seeking answers for your concerns and desires. Ask Him to help you seek His kingdom and His righteousness first.

KEYS PART 2

KEY 3: STRIVE FOR CONTENTMENT

In prayer, we must constantly perform a self-investigation to determine whether what we are asking for is a good desire or an illegitimate desire. Is my request pleasing in God's eyes or based in pride, lust, or ungratefulness?

Imagine it is Christmas morning for a moment. In your home, children are eagerly waiting for the opportunity to tear into their presents. If you are a parent, you know the frustration associated with watching your children tear open one gift to behold something they have desperately asked for, but before the wrapping has time to fall to the floor, they are already reaching for the next shiny package.

There's something like that in all of us. But if we are not truly grateful and content with what God has already provided, then why should He give us more to be ungrateful for? Blessings follow thanksgiving, not greed.

Is anything causing discontentment in your life today? Would you describe it as a need or a want?

Read Paul's instruction to Timothy, his son in the faith, in 1 Timothy 6:6-10. What did Paul tell Timothy should be enough to make him content?

With food and clothing, we should be content. Paul never described the type of food or the worth of the clothing. If we simply have those two things, we ought to be content. Paul is talking about our very basic needs.

Read Hebrews 13:5-6. What do these verses call us to do?

Based on these verses, what do we have that will never be taken away from us?

We are called to be satisfied with what we have. While that process can be difficult, here is the secret: Remember that God is your helper. We have the promise of His presence always. He is not a distant helper. He is intimately aware of all our cares and concerns. Jesus is our High Priest who stepped out of heaven to walk in flesh and He can sympathize with our weaknesses (Heb. 4:15). This is why the writer of Hebrews says:

Therefore let us draw near with confidence to the throne of grace, so that we may receive mercy and find grace to help in time of need.
HEBREWS 4:16

Today, in your time of prayer, focus on these things:
1. God, make my soul content.
2. Thank You for what You have already given me.
3. Remind me of the sufficiency of Your presence in my life.

Approach God's throne with boldness today. He is ever present and ready to help at the proper time. His time line doesn't always look like ours, but we can be assured that He will always provide.

KEY 4: MAKE A HABIT

We are hoping that these practices you have learned will continue in your own life far beyond this study. Hopefully, these truths from God's Word are creating habits in your life that will change you forever!

We have covered much ground in Scripture to discover what the Bible teaches regarding the practice of prayer.

Read and be encouraged by the Scripture passages below concerning the power of prayer:

14 If My people who are called by My name will humble themselves, and pray and seek My face, and turn from their wicked ways, then I will hear from heaven, and will forgive their sin and heal their land. 15 Now My eyes will be open and My ears attentive to prayer made in this place.
2 CHRONICLES 7:14-15, NKJV

The Lord is near to all who call upon Him,
To all who call upon Him in truth.
PSALM 145:18

The Lord is far from the wicked,
But He hears the prayer of the righteous.
PROVERBS 15:29

Therefore, confess your sins to one another, and pray for one another so that you may be healed. The effective prayer of a righteous man can accomplish much.
JAMES 5:16

Answer me when I call,
O God of my righteousness!
You have relieved me in my distress;
Be gracious to me and hear my prayer.
PSALM 4:1

What action words are used in those verses to describe our relationship to God in prayer?

What action words are used to describe God's response to His children who pray and call on Him?

Aren't you glad prayer is a two-way conversation? Our cries do not go up to a god of stone who doesn't hear and doesn't care. Our Father lives, loves, and listens. He hears His children and is near to those who call on Him. He is able to answer any request and willingly helps those who genuinely call upon Him in faith.

PRAYER STRATEGY TARGET

Finally, today you get to put pen to paper on the Prayer Strategy Target.

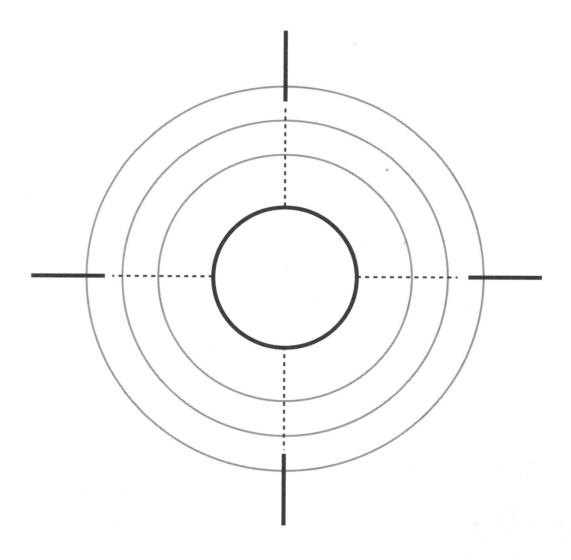

For this week and the remaining Day 5's moving forward we are going to start to fill in the slots around the target. You will notice that each target has 12 spaces to write and then 1 space to write in the middle. The middle is where you write the name of the person(s) for whom you are praying. But, around the name(s), you want to write what you are praying for them. Some of the spaces may stay the same from person to person. Other spaces will change for each person you are praying about. Today and the next few Prayer Strategy Days we will talk about the specifics that you may pray about for everyone. We will give you six ideas total over these next couple of weeks.

General Characteristic #1: Pray that this person loves and obeys God.

If someone loves Jesus and obeys Him, so many other things will fall into place. Imagine telling your children to go clean their messy rooms. Two hours later you walk in and see them in a circle on the floor, holding hands, praying for God to reveal His will about whether they should begin. You hear them asking Him to give them the spirit of cleanliness, to equip them with everything needed to straighten up what's so dirty and out of order.

Lofty prayers, but no submission. Rebellion wrapped in intercession. How would you react to that? You'd likely tell them to stop the performance and get busy doing what you'd already told them to do. Praying more is clearly not what they need to be doing at the moment. Obedience is.

But that's how a lot of people handle prayer. They hide behind it. They hope it will cover for disobedience in other areas that are a lot harder and more costly to do than just praying. God keeps telling them to do things, but they keep "praying about it" with no steps of action.

A lifestyle of obedience—while not a condition that earns salvation—is a major key to answered prayer. If you have a child who listens and obeys you, and another who ignores you and rebels, to which child are you more likely to give what he or she requests? Why should anyone call Jesus "Lord, Lord" if they're not serious about doing what He says (Luke 6:46)?

The logic couldn't be more clear. And Jesus couldn't have said it more plainly: "If you love Me, you will keep My commandments" (John 14:15). We're not saying we're capable of always doing things perfect, but how can we argue with His statement? To not follow Him with faith and submission while claiming total allegiance is the same as saying our love for Him is a cup of lukewarm coffee at best.

Obedience matters. Not in a legalistic way. Not as a means of pride or comparison with others. But life as a follower of Christ was never meant to be a casual attempt at doing as little as necessary—just enough to get by, just enough to feel good about going to church on Sunday morning. A person who is truly in Christ is steadily moving in a direction of greater obedience to Him.

> *3 And everyone who has this hope fixed on Him purifies himself, just as He is pure … 7 the one who practices righteousness is righteous, just as He is righteous.*
> **1 JOHN 3:3,7**

General Characteristic #2: Pray that this person follows God's commands.

The Bible is a gift to us. It teaches us about God, what is important to Him, what we need to do in response, how to live our life, and so much more.

If you are praying for a person to fall in love with God's Word and obey His commandments that are found there, then you are praying a powerful prayer. There is nothing more important than loving God with all that we are. It is the greatest of all commandments and why we are here on the earth.

SESSION 5
SPIRITUAL WARFARE

This week may have been tough. It isn't easy learning the ways we have put locks on our prayer life. But we pray the keys offered hope. We can't wait to hear how God uses the study of locks and keys to change lives.

Discuss the following questions from your personal study together as a group.

Using Philippians 4:8, make a list as a group of things you should think of when feeling anxious.

What does it look like to be content? Is contentment something you have a difficult time with? Why or why not? (Day 4)

Read Philippians 4:11-13. What does Paul indicate is the secret to learning contentment?

What are you learning about prayer from your Prayer Strategy Target work on this (and previous weeks)? Do you have any insights you've learned about the Prayer Strategy Target that you'd like to share with the group?

Share with the group the most important truth about prayer you have learned in this study so far.

Look back at your requests on page 9. Can anyone share an answered prayer from their list?

SESSION 5

VIDEO NOTES

_____
_____
_____
_____
_____
_____
_____
_____
_____
_____
_____
_____
_____
_____
_____
_____
_____
_____
_____
_____
_____
_____
_____
_____
_____
_____
_____

Video sessions are available for download at _www.lifeway.com/BattlePlan_

Watch The Session 5 Video and discuss the following questions with your group.

What were the most important points for you personally during this video session?

Talk about the names of the Devil. What do they say about him?

What are the enemy's three goals? (John 10:10) How have you seen the Devil use these three goals in your own life or lives of friends/churches/neighbors?

How can you apply the five second rule to your thought life?

How do you think the Devil responds when we really focus on prayer?

Compare James 4:6-8 and 1 Peter 5:6-11. What do these two passages teach you about the Devil? What do they instruct believers to do instead of allowing the Devil to defeat them?

Think about the seven parts of the R.E.S.P.O.N.D. acronym. Which of the seven comes easiest to you? Which is the hardest? Is there one you've never thought of before?

Pray together as a group for God to help you to R.E.S.P.O.N.D. well, walk in victory over the Devil, and stand firm in your faith when you are attacked by him.

IDENTIFYING THE ENEMY

To know how to pray in this battle, we must be aware of whom we are fighting.

We have a real Enemy. Our culture has made the Devil a comical costumed figure, but he is not an adversary that should be ignored or underestimated.

Satan is called the ruler of this world (John 16:11). He is described as exercising authority over the lower heavens, working in the lives of the disobedient (Eph. 2:2). Unbelievers are characterized as being held in the domain of darkness (Col. 1:13) by the power of Satan as he blinds their eyes so that they cannot see the light of the gospel (2 Cor. 4:3-4). He is the deceiver of the whole world as it is currently under his sway (1 John 5:19).

Satan uses windows of opportunity to steal, kill, and destroy (John 10:10). He approaches God in order to make accusations against us (Rev. 12:10). His original temptation caused Adam and Eve to doubt God's word. He is bold enough to afflict righteous Job (Job 1:9-12), ask to sift Peter (Luke 22:31), torment Paul (2 Cor. 12:7), and tempt Jesus Himself (Luke 4:1,13).

Knowing this, do you think Satan is intimidated to engage you in battle? Are you aware of his schemes in your life?

In the Book of Revelation, Satan's demise is promised. Read the description in Revelation 12:7-12 and underline key phrases that describe what Satan does and what will happen to him.

7 And there was war in heaven, Michael and his angels waging war with the dragon. The dragon and his angels waged war, 8 and they were not strong enough, and there was no longer a place found for them in heaven. 9 And the great dragon was thrown down, the serpent of old who is called the devil and Satan, who deceives the whole world; he was thrown down to the earth, and his angels were thrown down with him. 10 Then I heard a loud voice in heaven, saying, "Now the salvation, and the power, and the kingdom of our God and the authority of His Christ have come, for the accuser of our brethren has been thrown down, he who accuses them before our God day and night. 11 And they overcame him because of the blood of the Lamb and because of the word of their testimony, and they did not love their life even when faced with death. 12 For this reason, rejoice, O heavens and you who dwell in them. Woe to the earth and the sea, because the devil has come down to you, having great wrath, knowing that he has only a short time."

How does Satan try to deceive people today?

What might Satan use to accuse you before God?

What two things are given to us to be able to conquer him (v. 11)?

In your prayer time today, praise Jesus for His blood that silences the accusations of the deceiver. Your testimony of God's grace in your life sends the Enemy packing!

When Satan reminds you of what you have done, remind him of what Christ has done. Spend time thanking Jesus for salvation and praying against the Enemy's lying, scheming, deceiving ways in your life and the lives of those around you. Pray for discernment to see how he is attacking you and for courage to stand firm in your faith.

ARE YOU ON SATAN'S RADAR?

In yesterday's homework, we identified the real Enemy. We know about Satan. But here's a question for you: Does Satan know about you? Are you even on Satan's radar?

Read Acts 19:11-17 and underline key phrases as you read.

11 God was performing extraordinary miracles by the hands of Paul, 12 so that handkerchiefs or aprons were even carried from his body to the sick, and the diseases left them and the evil spirits went out. 13 But also some of the Jewish exorcists, who went from place to place, attempted to name over those who had the evil spirits the name of the Lord Jesus, saying, "I adjure you by Jesus whom Paul preaches." 14 Seven sons of one Sceva, a Jewish chief priest, were doing this. 15 And the evil spirit answered and said to them, "I recognize Jesus, and I know about Paul, but who are you?" 16 And the man, in whom was the evil spirit, leaped on them and subdued all of them and overpowered them, so that they fled out of that house naked and wounded. 17 This became known to all, both Jews and Greeks, who lived in Ephesus; and fear fell upon them all and the name of the Lord Jesus was being magnified..

In this passage, God was doing amazing things through the hands of Paul. Some traveling Jewish ministers were also attempting to exorcise demons from people.

When they tried to "use" the name of Jesus in their ministry, what did the demon say to them? What does this imply?

What did the demon do to them?

What does this passage teach us about winning spiritual battles?

The demons obviously knew about Jesus, but they were also fully aware of a missionary named Paul. He had done enough damage to their kingdom to get their attention.

But these seven sons of Sceva? They weren't even on the radar. No memos were posted about their lives. No concerns about their power.

They attempted to use the name of Jesus to perform miracles, but the evil spirit knew they did not belong to Christ. And without the power of Christ on their side, there was no hope that their ministry would succeed.

It begs the question: *Do the forces of hell know me by name?*

What are you doing to push back against Satan's forces?

Are you acting on your own strength or relying on the authority of Christ?

Spend time in prayer today and ask God to empower you in spiritual battles. Beg Him to keep your eyes alert to the Enemy around you. And ask Him to work holiness and power in your life so that you can stand firm against the tactics of the Devil (Eph. 6:11).

THE ARMOR OF GOD

To be able to fight well in spiritual warfare, we must rely on the teachings of Scripture and on the One who lives in us that is greater than the one who is in the world.

Paul teaches that to fight spiritual battles, we must put on the armor of God.

Read Ephesians 6:10-17. Why do we put on the armor of God (v. 11)?

What are we at war with in this life (v.12)?

Keep in mind that putting on the armor of God is not a battlefield technique, but a preparation technique. Paul is urging believers to take on the full armor of God in order to be prepared for the day of battle. Then we will be able to stand strong. Don't wait until the battle is raging to gird yourself with the protection of the armor of God.

Let's take a look at this armor in more detail. There are six pieces of armor named in verses 14-17. List each one, describing what these items are to look like in your life.

1.
2.
3.
4.
5.
6.

Which piece of armor are you employing the most right now? Is there a weak place in your armor that you need the Lord to strengthen?

Continuing on in Ephesians 6, we will see what Paul instructs is essential after one has put on the armor of God. Read Ephesians 6:18-20 and answer the questions that follow.

We are commanded to pray throughout the entire battle. What do you think Paul means when he says to pray "in the Spirit"?

To pray in the Spirit is to be inspired and led to pray by God's Holy Spirit (Rom. 8:14-16). When we are right with the Lord and surrendered to Him, His Spirit will fill us and lead us to cry out to God and pray for specific things and to pray specific verses back to God (Rom. 8:26-27).

What did Paul ask the people to pray for concerning him (vv. 19-20)?

After explaining how to put on the armor of God to prepare for battle against the Enemy, Paul asked for prayers for boldness. The same missionary who penned the words, "I am not ashamed of the gospel" (Rom. 1:16) still asked for others to pray for him so that he could fight well in the battle. He also asked for people to pray that God would open doors to share the gospel with others (Col. 4:3). He was rallying prayer support so that he could fight against the schemes of the Devil in his life and in his ministry.

If Paul asked for others to pray that for him, why wouldn't we pray that for ourselves? We all have shared prayer requests before—we pray for the sick, for jobs, for family, or for those who have lost a loved one. These things are wonderful and needed topics of prayer. But how often do we ask for people to pray for us that we would be bold in sharing the gospel?

Who in your life needs to hear the gospel?

What people of prayer could you send a message to right now and ask that they would pray you would be bold to share the gospel?

This not only provides prayer support but it also provides accountability. Send out those messages and then pray that God will open up a door for you and that you will walk through it with boldness when it is opened.

TAKE EVERY THOUGHT CAPTIVE

Begin today by reading 2 Corinthians 10:3-5 and make notes of important phrases or words.

What phrases grabbed your attention and why?

What do you think it means to take "every thought captive to the obedience of Christ"?

Just like the spiritual battles we fight are unseen, some of our most difficult struggles are inside our own minds: pride, insecurity, fear, distrust, doubt, worry. Sometimes our closest friends, even a spouse, may not know our deepest, most troubling thoughts. But the Lord knows.

Read Hebrews 4:12-13.

The Word of God is the tool to know if our heart is in line with His, to know if our thoughts are under His authority. We cannot take up physical arms to fight spiritual battles. We must learn to fight these battles on our knees. Through the weapon of prayer, we can demolish internal strongholds—lies Satan tells us to separate us from God's truth.

What kinds of strongholds could Satan be attempting to establish in your life?

What kinds of strongholds could Satan be attempting to establish in the lives of those closest to you?

The struggles are real. Instead of testing out all physical options, attempting frivolous arguments, or garnering all the professional help we can find, have we honestly prayed that the dominion of darkness would be thwarted? Have we prayed that these strongholds be broken down in the name of Jesus? Remember, prayer is not our last line of defense, it our only line of defense.

Read James 4:7. According to this verse, what is the solution for spiritual victory over the Devil?

Finish your time today by praying for spiritual victories over these spiritual strongholds. Submit to God in prayer and ask Him to take captive every thought so that you may be fully obedient to Him. Lift up the words of the final petition of Jesus' model prayer: "And do not lead us into temptation, but deliver us from evil" (Matt. 6:13).

PRAYER STRATEGY TARGET

We will continue our Prayer Strategy Day today talking about a few other general characteristics that you can pray over any person regardless of where they are in their life. Last week we hit:

General Characteristic #1: Pray that this person loves and obeys God.
General Characteristic #2: Pray that this person follows God's commands.

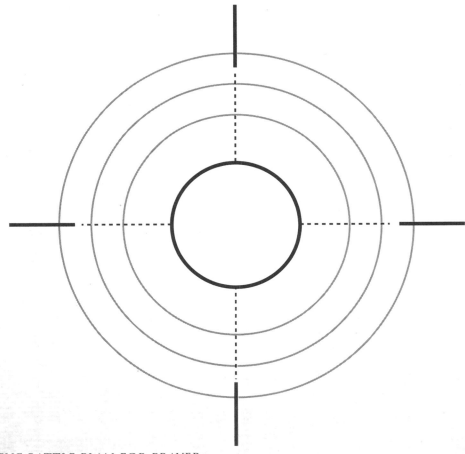

Today we will hit two more characteristics.

General Characteristic #3: Pray that this person will love and serve others.

Consider 1 Peter 4:8-11:

> *8 Above all, keep fervent in your love for one another, because love covers a multitude of sins. 9 Be hospitable to one another without complaint. 10 As each one has received a special gift, employ it in serving one another as good stewards of the manifold grace of God. 11 Whoever speaks, is to do so as one who is speaking the utterances of God; whoever serves is to do so as one who is serving by the strength which God supplies; so that in all things God may be glorified through Jesus Christ, to whom belongs the glory and dominion forever and ever. Amen.*

Above all, love each other deeply. What a challenge. It isn't always easy, but what a payoff if we do. We should be known by our love for one another so as you are praying, pray that this person would love and serve others.

General Characteristic #4: Pray that this person will have faith instead of doubt.

When you pray, you should rest in the fact that God is not unaware, unable, uncaring, unwilling, or unlikely to answer. That's why He keeps prompting you to ask in faith. Your heart can be right with God and with others, and yet your doubts during prayer can create roadblocks.

Peter, for example, unnecessarily denied Jesus three times. Sometimes we, too, might quietly deny God's faithfulness, goodness, or ability in our hearts when we approach Him. This lack of faith will clog up your prayer life. You'll quit wanting to come close to God if you don't trust Him or believe He is good.

So, when you are praying for others, pray that they would trust in God's faithfulness. Take Him at His word and believe that He understands their needs and is able to help.

Next week in Day 5 we will look at the final two characteristics we can pray for anyone.

PRAYING IN FAITH

Welcome to Session 6! This week, you learned about spiritual warfare in your personal study. We hope this doesn't scare you, but makes you aware of the constant battle for your heart. But we can rejoice, knowing the One who wins the war!

Is spiritual warfare something you've thought about a lot? Why or why not?

What is something new or interesting you learned in this week's personal study?

Read Ephesians 6:14-17 together as a group. There are six pieces of armor named. List each one, describing what each looks like in your life, or in the life of someone you know. (Day 3)

What do you think it means to take "every thought captive to the obedience of Christ"? (Day 4)

SESSION 6

VIDEO NOTES

_____

_____

_____

_____

_____

_____

_____

_____

_____

_____

_____

_____

_____

_____

_____

_____

_____

_____

_____

_____

_____

_____

_____

_____

Video sessions are available for download at _www.lifeway.com/BattlePlan_

Watch the video for Session 6 and discuss the following as a group.

What were the most important points for you personally during this video session?

We looked at Matthew 21:22 and James 1:6-8 quickly in the video this session. Spend a few minutes unpacking those Scriptures with your group and discuss what it means to pray in faith. How have you seen that played out in your life or the lives of others?

"God loves to get caught in a promise"—how does that help you in pray in faith?

Do you think God is working on answering your future prayers? Does that help you pray in faith? Does it keep you from praying? Why or why not?

What do you think of God's perfect track record? How does that help you when you come to Him in prayer?

Read Mark 11:20-26. What does this passage teach about praying in faith?

What are some key passages or things God has done in your past that could strengthen your faith to remember as you pray?

Look over page 9 and discuss any answered prayers in your lives. Pray now for one another and ask God to develop an incredible faith in His love and power to answer your requests.

DAY 1

OUR FATHER IS ABLE

Understanding the identity of our Father is a foundational principle concerning prayer.

God's Word is our best source to remedy our inadequate understanding concerning our Heavenly Father. This week, we will counteract common misconceptions concerning God. The more we understand God's character and how He interacts with His children, the more confident we will be in our prayers.

MISCONCEPTION #1: GOD IS UNABLE

Let's study what God's Word says about our Heavenly Father.

Under each verse, make notes about what it teaches concerning the character of God. Pray as you go through these Scriptures. Sometimes we can learn a bunch of information about God and forget to pray to Him. Let's keep the prayer going.

Yet for us there is but one God, the Father, from whom are all things and we exist for Him.
1 CORINTHIANS 8:6A

While this verse clearly tells us that all things are from God, what are some specific things He has given you? Write those down and thank God for them.

When the Scripture says, "we exist for Him," what does that mean practically in your work, your family, etc.? Commit those areas of your life to Him in prayer.

One God and Father of all who is over all and through all and in all.
EPHESIANS 4:6

Your Father is over all. In what ways are you thankful for this aspect of God?

He is able to do all things because He is over all things. Praise Him for His sovereignty and authority.

Blessed be the God and Father of our Lord Jesus Christ, who has blessed us with every spiritual blessing in the heavenly places in Christ.
EPHESIANS 1:3

What are the spiritual blessings with which God has blessed you? Write them down and thank your Father for these gifts (forgiveness of sins, spiritual gifts, etc.).

Close in prayer by thanking your generous Father for who He is and what He has done. He is the only God. All things come from Him and exist for Him. He is above all things. He has blessed us with every spiritual blessing. Thank Him that He is able to do above and beyond anything we could ask or think (Eph. 3:20).

OUR FATHER IS CARING

MISCONCEPTION #2: GOD IS UNCARING

Many people interpret negative circumstances in their lives incorrectly, believing that God does not care enough about them to get involved. Scripture paints a completely different picture of our Father.

Children want to be able to trust that their parents will continually care for them—that they will come through in their time of greatest need. You may or may not be able to say that about your earthly father, but you can be confident in the steadfastness of your Heavenly Father. Today, we are going to thank God for His consistency and care in our lives.

Read Psalm 68:5 and notice how the psalmist describes our Father.

Holy means *set apart*. It is different. Better. Special. Unique. This verse tells us that God has a set apart dwelling place. It is a place where He chooses and desires to dwell (Ps. 68:16). Many people think God is unaware of their everyday lives. Believing that He is too lofty or too out-of-touch with us down here on earth, some people will live in such a way that ignores God's involvement in their lives. They ignore God because they believe that God is ignoring them. Yet even from His holy place, God cares for those in need.

According to Psalm 68:5, what two groups of people does God show concern for from His holy dwelling?

What does that teach us about His character?

The Bible teaches us that God knows how many hairs are upon our heads (Luke 12:7), He collects our tears in a bottle (Ps. 56:8), and He promises to supply all of our needs (Phil. 4:19). God is not unaware; He is not uncaring.

Read Isaiah 64:8 and notice how aware and involved God is in your life.

But now, O Lord, You are our Father,
We are the clay, and You our potter;
And all of us are the work of Your hand.
ISAIAH 64:8

God has created you and sustained you in a unique way. God created you and wrote every one of your days down in a book before anyone else had a chance to crack open the cover.

Thank God for how He has created you and how He has sustained you. Before moving on, take time to praise Him for how He fearfully and wonderfully made you (Ps. 139:14).

Read Matthew 7:9-11. According to these verses, how is our heavenly Father different from our earthly fathers?

James also reminds believers about the greater nature of gifts given by God compared to the lesser value of offerings given by the world.

Read James 1:17:

Every good thing given and every perfect gift is from above, coming down from the Father of lights, with whom there is no variation or shifting shadow.

What are 3 good things or perfect gifts that God has given you?
1.
2.
3.
What does it mean that there is "no variation" with our Father?

Thank God for His care and awareness in your life. Be honest with Him concerning your needs acknowledging that He is near and available to help. What is your greatest care today? Cast it on your loving Father and eagerly wait to see how He responds.

OUR FATHER IS CONCERNED

MISCONCEPTION #3: GOD IS UNCONCERNED

While some people struggle with the idea that God is unaware of our difficult situations, many people struggle in a different way. Some believe that God is unconcerned with our choices. If we believe God to be too distant or too soft to concern Himself with our lifestyle, we can slip into complacency and unholy living.

Make no mistake—God is not mocked (Gal. 6:7). He is concerned with your situation, but He is also concerned with your lifestyle.

Look how our Father is described in Deuteronomy 32:6.

> *Is this how you repay the LORD, you foolish and senseless people? Isn't He your Father and Creator? Didn't He make you and sustain you?*
> **DEUTERONOMY 32:6, HCSB**

In this passage, the people of God were not acting like the people of God. They were foolish and senseless in their decisions and this type of thinking was leading them to live unholy lives. The absurdity of their actions was pitted against the character of God. How could the people act like this if they had such a Father?

What is important about God being our Father that should cause us to think carefully about how we live?

God is not only concerned with how we live, but He is a Father who cares enough that He will step in and stop us when we go too far. He is a Father who disciplines His children!

Read Hebrews 12:9-11 and discover something about the concerned nature of our Father.

9 Furthermore, we had earthly fathers to discipline us, and we respected them; shall we not much rather be subject to the Father of spirits, and live? 10 For they disciplined us for a short time as seemed best to them, but He disciplines us for our good, so that we may share His holiness. 11 All discipline for the moment seems not to be joyful, but sorrowful; yet to those who have been trained by it, afterwards it yields the peaceful fruit of righteousness.
HEBREWS 12:9-11

What methods did your parents use to discipline you?

Even though it was difficult to receive, what benefit did you gain from their discipline?

How do you think God disciplines us? What methods does He use?

What is God's goal in disciplining us?

God's wrath is designated for unbelievers. God's discipline is designated for believers. The way to avoid wrath is to receive Christ. The way to avoid discipline is to obey Christ.

Pray and ask God if there are some things He wants you to stop doing or start doing. Commit these items to Him in prayer and submit to our loving Heavenly Father.

OUR FATHER IS FORGIVING

MISCONCEPTION #4: GOD IS UNFORGIVING

We sometimes imagine God to be as petty as we are. Assuming He holds grudges due to previous mistakes, sometimes our prayers are stifled because we believe He doesn't want to hear from us.

While our Father is diligent to discipline us, He is also eager to pardon us. He loves to show compassion to His children. Do you remember the parable of the Prodigal Son?

The younger son asked for his part of his inheritance and squandered it in reckless living (Luke 15:13). When he hit rock bottom and came to his senses, he reasoned to himself: "I will get up and go to my father, and will say to him, 'Father, I have sinned against heaven, and in your sight; I am no longer worthy to be called your son; make me as one of your hired men'" (Luke 15:18-19).

As he made the long and humbling trip back home, can you imagine the scenarios that were running through his mind?

How could this man's father have responded?

Willing to accept the consequences and assume a demoted role with his father, he went home. But instead of condemnation and speeches filled with, "I told you so's," read how this father reacted in Luke 15:20.

> *So he got up and came to his father. But while he was still*
> *a long way off, his father saw him and felt compassion for*
> *him, and ran and embraced him and kissed him.*
> **LUKE 15:20**

What words surprise you in this verse? Why?

This father was eagerly longing for his son's return. Seeing him from afar, this father, filled with compassion, could not walk to his son—he ran to his son! Overwhelmed with joy, he passionately threw his arms around his son's neck and showered him with kisses.

This is not a picture of an unforgiving, detached father. This is a picture of our Father in heaven who longs for our return and rejoices when we come to our senses.

How does this image change the way you view your Heavenly Father?

As the nation of Israel emerged from 40 years of wilderness wanderings, Moses reminded the people of how God had persevered with them. See how God is portrayed among the people of Israel before they entered the promised land:

> *30 The Lord your God who goes before you will Himself fight on your behalf, just as He did for you in Egypt before your eyes, 31 and in the wilderness where you saw how the Lord your God carried you, just as a man carries his son, in all the way which you have walked until you came to this place.*
> **DEUTERONOMY 1:30-31**

What is so encouraging in this depiction of our Father?

Today, spend time thanking our Father for running to us with compassion. Thank Him for fighting for us when all our strength is gone. Thank Him for the way He carried us to this point in our lives. Spend time expressing your love and gratitude to our Father.

PRAYER STRATEGY TARGET

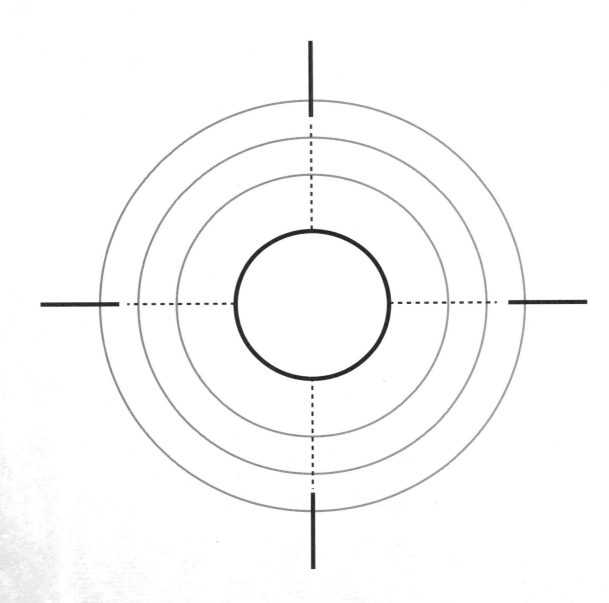

Before we continue our Prayer Strategy Target work, let's recall the four general characteristics we discussed previously:

General Characteristic #1: Pray that this person loves and obeys God.

General Characteristic #2: Pray that this person follows God's commands.

General Characteristic #3: Pray that this person will love and serve others.

General Characteristic #4: Pray that this person will have faith instead of doubt.

Now, onto the last two general characteristics. Remember, though, these are not the only things you need to pray for every person. There are many other ones to consider, but our hope is that these six get you started.

General Characteristic #5: Pray for the fruit of the Spirit to be manifested in this person's life.

22 But the fruit of the Spirit is love, joy, peace, patience, kindness, goodness, faithfulness, 23 gentleness, self-control; against such things there is no law. 24 Now those who belong to Christ Jesus have crucified the flesh with its passions and desires. 25 If we live by the Spirit, let us also walk by the Spirit.

GALATIANS 5:22-25

These qualities and characteristics flow out of a person who is connected to God. These are what God produces in a person who follows after Him. Pray that the person would stay connected to the Lord and that this fruit would flow freely in his/her life. Pray that the person would have peace through Christ Jesus. Pray that the person would have self-control in his/her life. Pray that the life of this person is marked by kindness and goodness. This is what God wants for each believer, so pray it along with Him!

General Characteristic #6: Pray the Lord's Prayer over this person.

As you think about how to really target this kind of praying, consider a strategy that actually works for all kinds of different settings and different people: using the Lord's Prayer as an outline. Instead of praying it for yourself, pray it for your fellow believers. Something like this:

> *Father in heaven, I pray for my brother (my sister), praising Your name for them, asking You to fill their heart with worship for You today. Help them to honor Your name above themselves. May their primary desire always be to advance Your kingdom, wherever they happen to be, whatever they happen to be doing.*
>
> *May they align themselves on the earth with Your will, just as surely as Your will is followed and accomplished in heaven. Provide them, I pray, with their daily bread—with everything You know is required for them to thrive and be cared for. And grant them repentance, forgiving them of their sins—even as You forgive me of mine—while also keeping their relationships free from bitterness and difficulty as they forgive those who've sinned against them.*
>
> *Please, Lord, protect them from temptation, from allowing them to be overloaded with adversity. And deliver them from all evil—from every scheme and attack of the Enemy, from every weapon intended to defeat and discourage them. For Yours, Lord, is the kingdom, the power, the glory, forever. You reign and rule and have already given them victory through the finished work of Christ. So I pray for them today, and I pray in His name. Amen.*

Now that's strategically targeting a prayer. That's biblical praying. That's using the Word—and where appropriate, using your specific knowledge of the person—to aim a prayer in such a way that it covers all aspects of their life and seeks God's will for every bit of it. Use the space provided to write a prayer of your own.

_____

_____

_____

_____

_____

_____

_____

_____

_____

_____

_____

_____

_____

_____

_____

_____

_____

_____

_____

_____

_____

_____

_____

_____

Next week, we will not have a Prayer Strategy Target, but we will be learning methods we can use to pray every day in Week 8 and beyond this study.

SESSION 7

PRAYING SPECIFICALLY AND STRATEGICALLY

Praying in faith is essential and we hope you learned much this past week about who God is and how He wants us to approach Him in prayer.

Did you relate to any of the misconceptions listed this week? If you're comfortable doing so, share which ones you've struggled with most and why.

What evidence have you seen that God is able? (Day 1)

What does it mean to be holy? How does understanding God's holiness affect the way you feel about His care for you? (Day 2)

How have you learned from discipline in the past? What is God's goal in disciplining us? (Day 3)

What stands out to you in the story of the prodigal son? How does that encourage your understanding of God as our Father? (Day 4)

SESSION 7

VIDEO NOTES

_____

_____

_____

_____

_____

_____

_____

_____

_____

_____

_____

_____

_____

_____

_____

_____

_____

_____

_____

_____

_____

_____

_____

_____

_____

_____

_____

_____

Video sessions are available for download at _www.lifeway.com/BattlePlan_

Watch the Session 7 video and discuss the following with your group.

What were the most important points for you personally during this video session?

In this session we talk about praying specifically and strategically. Share a time in your life where you either prayed specifically or strategically and the result of that time in prayer.

Praying God's Word can be a powerful thing. How have you prayed God's Word in the past? Any tips you want to share with the group? Or what did this particular video inspire in you as it pertains to praying God's Word?

As an exercise in praying God's Word—take Psalm 91 and unpack it together with your group, writing down specific items you can pray for and take time to do so together in your group. Adapt it, making the pronouns personal.

Let's get specific as we move into our final week of study. Pick a person you and your group want to pray for together as a team. Start to make a list of specific things you want to pray for that person. Feel free to use the Word of God to help you. Make a list and spend some time praying specifically. Take turns praying together for this person during your group time. Allow God's Spirit to guide what you pray.

The Lord delights in answering your requests. However, we know there are times when you have been praying for something for a long time and have not seen that answer come to pass. If you feel comfortable, bring that concern to your group and pray together for that need. Also, be encouraged to keep bringing that prayer to God. His timing is perfect.

Share any answered prayer from page 9. Use Ephesians 1:15-19 to pray specifically for one another as a group.

PRAYING SCRIPTURE

There is power packed into God's Word. Unfortunately, for many of us, the practice of blending prayer with the reading of Scripture remains unexplored.

If your heart is right with God and others and you are ready to pray, then what should guide your praying? True, prayer can flow directly from your heart. No script is necessary. Nothing prescribed or recited. Prayer is personal. Completely unique. Yet even with this much freedom involved, God does provide powerful resources to help us pray strategically and specifically. To help you know for certain that your heart is beating in step with God's.

Perhaps the first and most comprehensive guide of all is to pray to God using the very words He's already spoken in His Word. We humans are fickle. Hot and cold. Moods and emotions that flame within us today can be nearly forgotten memories by the end of the week. But when we pray with words and thoughts that are inspired by Scripture, we're assured that our praying is anchored in bedrock truths that stretch back centuries. They keep our praying steadfast and consistent.

You may think, *Well, I don't know the Bible enough. I wouldn't know where to start.* That is not a problem, you can even pray about that too. God will guide you as you seek Him.

Praying God's Word means reading or reciting Scripture in an attitude and spirit of prayer. We let the meaning of the verses become our prayer. These scriptural prayers encourage, inspire, and transform our minds and hearts.

> **Instead of picking verses randomly, try praying Scripture prayers to start. Read the following Scripture prayers from the New Testament and make a quick note about what each one is about.**
> **Acts 4:24-30**
>
> **Philippians 1:9-11**
>
> **Colossians 1:9-14**

1 Thessalonians 3:11-13

Hebrews 13:20-21

Revelation 4:8,11

Revelation 5:9-10

Which one speaks most to your situation and circumstances right now?

Read that specific passage as your own and change some pronouns if needed. What jumps out as especially relevant to you?

Write down the passage again as a prayer and dwell on each word and its meaning. Let it inspire and shape your prayer.

Does it lead you to pray other prayers of confession, repentance, or praise? Are you challenged to pursue a new act of obedience?

As you pray Scripture what is your takeaway? How will you put this scriptural truth into practice today?

See, that wasn't too difficult, was it? If you start to put praying Scripture into practice, we know that it will bear much fruit in your life.

Now pray and ask God to prompt you with specific verses to pray at specific times. Ask Him to empower you with His Spirit and help you to pray in faith and trust His Word as you go through your day.

PRAYING GOD'S NAMES

Dr. John Smith is called different names at different times. His father calls him "Son"; his wife calls him "Sweetheart"; his patients call him "Doc"; and his friends at church call him "Brother Jack." At the hospital he's "the doctor with the best bedside manner," and the waiters at a local restaurant refer to him as "that happy Christian who leaves good tips." John isn't multiple people. He's one man with multiple roles and character traits.

Each of John's names or titles reveals a little more about who he is, what he does, and how he relates to others. In like manner, the Bible reveals that our one God has many names. When we pray to Him, we may come to Him for a wide variety of reasons. Because He is eternal and limitless, the many titles and descriptions used of Him in the Bible are vast and astounding. But that's the point. Each name of God helps us to understand, value, and worship Him even more.

Unlike the Egyptians and Greeks who prayed to different mythical gods depending upon their need, we worship one God who alone is living and limitless, Maker and Master, holy and most high, Savior and sovereign of all, and everything we need in all circumstances. As we discover and get familiar with different names of God, we not only better recognize God for who He is, but we can relate to Him more personally and intimately.

We are going to explore just a few of God's many names today and discuss how to pray using the names of God as our backbone.

Psalm 91:1-2 describes God by saying, "He who dwells in the secret place of the Most High shall abide under the shadow of the Almighty. I will say of the Lord, 'He is my refuge and my fortress; My God, in Him I will trust'" (NKJV). In these two verses, the same God is referred to by multiple names and descriptions: Elyon (the Most High), Shaddai (the Almighty), Yahweh (the Lord), my refuge, my fortress, and my God (Elohim).

As you consider each of these names and descriptions below, make notes about the significance of each one based upon Psalm 91:1-2.

1. Elyon (the Most High):

2. Shaddi (the Almighty):

3. Yahweh (the Lord):

4. Elohim (my refuge or fortress):

Yesterday we discussed praying God's Word. Today we are discussing the names of God. Let's combine the two together and try something. Below we've listed some names of God and some Scripture references. Take a few minutes and look up the Scripture passage identified for each name and write a prayer out to God thanking Him for these attributes and characteristics.

1. The Eternal God - Isaiah 40:28

2. The God of All Comfort - 2 Corinthians 1:3

3. The King of Heaven - Daniel 4:37

4. The Lord of Peace - 2 Thessalonians 3:16

5. The Light of the World - John 8:12

These are just a few of the names of God and Jesus in the Bible. Even if you don't remember any formal or Hebrew names of God, you can praise Him in your native language by calling out to Him as the God of love, faithfulness, mercy, comfort, protection, justice, forgiveness, power, and salvation. The list goes on and on.

The point is to seek Him, worship Him, and pray to Him for who He is. To acknowledge Him as the Creator, Your Father, and the One who is everything you need. His love for you is great, and your love for Him is reflected by your desire to know Him and obey Him.

So as you pray strategically, remember to call out to your God by His names as you learn them. He loves to hear His children acknowledge Him for all He does and all He can do. And doesn't He deserve it? After all, He is God our Salvation. "Let them praise the name of the LORD: for his name alone is excellent; his glory is above the earth and heaven" (Ps. 148:13, KJV).

And to that, we say, "Blessed be the name of the Lord!"

Pick out one of the verses from today. Meditate on that passage today—write it out, memorize it, think about it. Use that verse as you pray, thanking God for who He is.

DAY 3

PRAYING OFFENSIVELY

Part of a good prayer strategy is knowing how to pray against evil. We all know, of course, the dangers that lurk within temptation. We're well familiar with the Enemy's arrows of fear, anger, lust, and jealousy. But today we will focus on going on the offensive in a positive way — meaning praying for the advancement of love, life, and truth.

Sure, there are times when we need to play defense. But not all the time. We need a game plan for offense as well—asking God to open doors for the gospel, to send forth laborers into the harvest field, to pour out His Holy Spirit in revival, to fill us with His love and the knowledge of His will, to use our spiritual gifts in His service, and to raise up a generation who will honor His name. Spiritual warfare is about standing our ground against the Enemy and taking new ground for the kingdom.

> *Let your light shine before men in such a way that they may see*
> *your good works, and glorify your Father who is in heaven.*
> **MATTHEW 5:16**

Think of your marriage, family, or city and consider the answers these questions generate:

What could I pray for that would be overwhelmingly good and loving?

What could greatly advance God's kingdom in this situation and glorify Him?

We find positive prayers and steps for taking ground all through Scripture. In fact, God wants to help us and give us gifts along the way to encourage and assist us. Jesus tells us in Matthew 7:11, "If you then, being evil, know how to give good gifts to your children, how much more will your Father who is in heaven give what is good to those who ask Him!"

When we love someone, we want nothing but the best for them. John prays this type of prayer in 3 John 2, saying, "Beloved, I pray that in all respects you may prosper and be in good health, just as your soul prospers." If God is good and is preparing good things for us, then we need to be actively seeking and asking for these things.

Pray very loving prayers. We need to cover situations in prayer and ask God to bless, provide, and be glorified as much as possible … praying that He would do more than we can ask or imagine. Why? Because His glory is the ultimate goal of all praying.

Not to mention that one of the best defenses is a great offense. So don't just pray against hardship, but pray for blessings also. Instead of merely praying against a divorce, for instance, ask God to make your marriage a beautiful picture of the gospel of Christ and His love for His bride, and that He will use you to minister to others and advance the kingdom through your loving relationship as husband and wife.

Instead of praying that your church leaders won't fight during a business meeting, pray for loving unity and revival to break out, resulting in greater ministry opportunities.

Romans 12:21 says, "Do not be overcome by evil, but overcome evil with good." The apostle Paul was a great example of this mind-set when praying for his new brothers and sisters in the faith. He wrote in long, uplifting terms in Colossians 1:9-12:

> *9 We have not ceased to pray for you and to ask that you may be filled with the knowledge of His will in all spiritual wisdom and understanding, 10 so that you will walk in a manner worthy of the Lord, to please Him in all respects, bearing fruit in every good work and increasing in the knowledge of God; 11 strengthened with all power, according to His glorious might, for the attaining of all steadfastness and patience; joyously 12 giving thanks to the Father, who has qualified us to share in the inheritance of the saints in Light.*

Wouldn't you want something prayed over you like that? To be filled with knowledge, wisdom, and an understanding of God's will? To bear much fruit in your life for God's glory?

This is how to pray proactively and go on the offense. Pray for someone right now in your family. Ask for God's richest blessings upon their life.

DAY 4

PRAYING PREEMPTIVELY

If you were the leader of a country and discovered that you would soon be attacked by a brutal, invading army, what would you do? If no terms of peace were possible, you would do everything plausible to quickly prepare for war. Gathering resources. Stationing troops.

This is also what we must do in prayer. We must first fight our battles on our knees before the battle rages in the natural realm. Let's spend some time today looking at the Enemy's playbook so we can be preemptive in our prayer strategy.

DISTRACTION

Misdirection is Warfare 101. David wrote, "I am restless in my complaint and am surely distracted, because of the voice of the enemy" (Ps. 55:2-3). Satan will constantly try to get you off track to focus on even good things which are not God's best things.

In what areas of your life are you prone to distraction? Spend a moment writing a prayer out to the Lord about focusing on God's best.

DECEPTION

Jesus said whenever Satan speaks a lie (which is all the time), "he speaks from his own nature, for he is a liar and the father of lies" (John 8:44). Strongholds, addictions, and sins are founded upon lies. They are a perversion of God's truth. Promises never delivered. False advertising.

Sin will fail you, let you down, and leave you empty. But Satan's temptations brazenly try to assure you that if you act now, your situation will be different. It won't affect you like it does other people. He displays the pleasure and hides the consequences. That's why you can't ever believe him.

In what areas of your life has deception taken hold? Spend a moment writing a prayer to God to help you in this area.

DERISION

When the Devil's not lying, he's usually running you down or running down someone else in your mind. Bringing up things from your past. Falsely presuming someone else's guilt. Yes, you've been forgiven in the blood of Christ, yet Satan keeps you scraping old wounds. Inciting doubt. He's the "accuser of our brethren" (Rev. 12:10)—accusing you of not being good enough, even though that's why Christ came in love to save you. In order for you to deflect these accusations, you need to be studying the Word, finding your identity in Christ, and praying for wisdom and discernment. That's how you throw out the Enemy's trumped-up charges.

Spend some moments praying preemptively against the derision and mockery that Satan may be trying to do in your life.

DIVISION

One hallmark of the gospel is the loving unity it brings to people of all nations, all backgrounds, all ages, and demographics. All in Christ. One in Christ. But Satan knows "if a house is divided against itself, that house will not be able to stand" (Mark 3:25). Anger and argument among God's people will not destroy the gospel, but they can destroy your testimony and effectiveness in sharing it. Disunity paints Christians and our faith as being weak and hypocritical. When husbands and wives are at odds, when children and their parents clash, when the pastor and his church quarrel, you can be sure the main culprit is actually the one you can't see. Stirring up division. Sowing discord among brethren Encouraging us to presume the worst instead of praying for the best.

We must not live foolishly "ignorant of [Satan's] schemes" (2 Cor. 2:11). We should pray for God to help us stay focused on His will, for His Holy Spirit to keep us walking in truth, for false accusations to be thrown down, and for love and unity to reign in our relationships.

In what ways is Satan trying to divide you? Pray against division and for unity in your family and church today.

PRAYING WISDOM

You will notice that we are not spending time on the Prayer Strategy Target today. That's because next week we will be incorporating the Strategy Target into every day of homework. For this last day of our week on praying specifically and strategically we are going to cover calling on God's wisdom in our prayer life.

"Wisdom is supreme—so get wisdom. And whatever else you get, get understanding" (Prov. 4:7, HCSB). Not many things in life come with this kind of endorsement. Whatever else you get. Whatever else you do. Yet anytime we hear this kind of ultimatum, we know something important is about to be said. And when God is the One who's making the proclamation through His Word, you can be sure His advice is worth heeding.

How often do you pray for God's wisdom in your life and in your decision-making process?

What is one upcoming decision or situation in which you need to pray for wisdom? List it here. (Feel free to list more than one if you feel led!)

Acquiring wisdom, God says, is of "supreme" importance. And prayer is one of the keys that unlocks it. In fact, prayer yields wisdom, and then wisdom yields better prayer. Wisdom is the ability to apply knowledge to a given situation. Making the best choices with the data you have. To take what you know and make it work really well. To make your relationships work. To make your money work. To make grand-slam, home-run decisions about friendship, marriage, and parenting.

Wisdom helps us discern what is right and good. It guides you to do the ethically right thing in the morally right way. It unlocks everything—things that used to seem like a mystery. When faced with dilemmas that once sent you swerving out of control, wisdom helps you locate the straight, sure path, so that "when you walk, your steps will not be impeded; And if you run, you will not stumble" (Prov. 4:12).

You'll be able to look back on vital moments of decision and see that you were protected from rashness and folly. Wisdom is what we need. It helps you see things from God's eternal perspective, understand the cause and effect of a decision, and constantly learn from any situation. And God, knowing this, promises to give wisdom to those who "ask" Him for it. That word in James 1:5 not only carries the idea of asking, but of begging, calling out for something, craving it. God promises to give wisdom "generously"— especially to those who "seek [it] as silver And search for [it] as for hidden treasures" (Prov. 2:4). We should want it, and want it badly.

He also says He'll give it "without reproach"—without insult or condescension (Jas. 1:5). Without making fun of us for being so foolish up until now. He wants us to win. He wants to give us what we need for being successful in our families, in our work, in everything we do—"bearing fruit in every good work and increasing in the knowledge of God" (Col. 1:10). Because this gives Him glory. As much as He's glorified through our spoken praise and worship, He is glorified also through our integrity, our honesty, our diligence, our humility, our purity, our faithfulness. He is glorified by our being good spouses, parents, employees, and stewards of our resources.

> **How does knowing that God longs to give you wisdom help you in the current situation you described earlier?**

For the LORD gives wisdom;
From His mouth come knowledge and understanding.
PROVERBS 2:6

As we close out our week, write a prayer to God using this verse and ask for wisdom in your life in whatever difficult circumstance comes to mind.

SESSION 8

PRAYER
STRATEGIES

This is our last week together. We are so excited to see you utilize all the tools we have studied as you learn to pray strategically and specifically.

Discuss the following questions from your personal study together as a group.

Have you prayed using Scripture before this week? What about God's names? What was new or different for you as you prayed this way? How did that help you in your prayers?

Think of your small group, church, and/or city and write down the answers these questions generate:
What is the most loving thing I can ask for right now?

What could I pray for that would be overwhelmingly good?

What could greatly advance God's Kingdom in this situation?

What could I pray for that would be really glorifying to God?

Together, use the answers from the questions above to pray over your group, your church, and your city. And know that this coming week in your personal study you will really put pen to paper on specific prayer strategies for people in your life.

SESSION 8

VIDEO NOTES

_____

_____

_____

_____

_____

_____

_____

_____

_____

_____

_____

_____

_____

_____

_____

_____

_____

_____

_____

_____

_____

_____

_____

_____

Video sessions are available for download at *www.lifeway.com/BattlePlan*

Watch the Session 8 video and discuss the following as a group.

What were the most important points for you personally during this video session?

What prayer strategies can you employ this week to pray for the lost?

Share with the group the name of someone you know who does not yet know Christ. Take time praying over those names in your group.

Make a list of people in your community to pray for as a group.

How can the group pray for you to be bold in your witness?

There are seven ways the Holy Spirit works listed in the video. Which ways have you seen?

Read Galatians 5:22-25 and Ephesians 5:18-21 and answer the question: What does it look like to be continually filled with the Holy Spirit?

Close in prayer and pray for one another using what you learned today.

PRAY FOR YOUR FAMILY

It's time to get specific. Let's start directing our prayers to develop an intentional battle plan for people in our lives. Oftentimes, we pray that all the family is safe, that God bless all the missionaries, and that there be peace on earth. Those are wonderful prayers, but we need to get specific. We want you to develop a list of those you are going to pray for and how. Some of these categories will be easy and some of these will be challenging.

Let's begin with your family. Regardless of your current family situation, each of us have people we consider family. It is easy to resort to worrying for our family or attempting to fix all of their situations, but are we strategically praying for them?

How often and in what ways are you currently praying for family members?

When King David was nearing his death, he prayed over the entire nation of Israel but eventually he focused his prayer specifically upon his family. For the whole nation to hear, this father prayed a special prayer concerning his son. Read 1 Chronicles 29:18-19 and notice what he asked of the Lord.

8 O Lord, the God of Abraham, Isaac and Israel, our fathers, preserve this forever in the intentions of the heart of Your people, and direct their heart to You; 19 and give to my son Solomon a perfect heart to keep Your commandments, Your testimonies and Your statutes, and to do them all, and to build the temple, for which I have made provision.
1 CHRONICLES 29:18-19

What are some of the specific things that David prayed for concerning his son, Solomon?

In the same way that David prayed targeted prayers for his son, we need to get specific concerning our prayer targets for our family. In the chart below, fill out the names of your family members and how you want to pray for each one of them. What pivotal prayers need to be offered up regarding each family member?

Do some research and find at least two or three Bible verses you can pray over each one as well. Scripture-saturated prayers (John 15:7) provide powerful clarity. You may have to do some work to find verses, but it will be worth the time. Whether you use a commentary, your Bible index, or an Internet search, find verses with which to target these prayers. In addition, select what days you want to pray for each family member. It may be every day or you may want to focus on certain family members on pivotal days.

Name	Prayer Needs	Verses to Pray	Days to Pray

As you close today, use the target on the next page and commit to praying targeted prayers for family every day this week. Each day of homework in this session will introduce a new group of people to target with your prayers. Like David, don't cease to pray for those in your care.

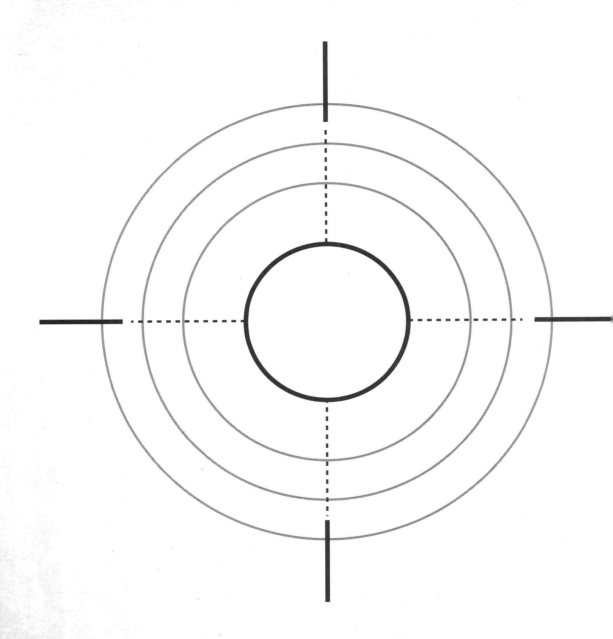

This week, we will have a Prayer Strategy Target each day. We'll provide specific points to pray for each person in that Day's lesson. Of course, remember some of the general prayers that could apply to anyone, but let's spend some time thinking about praying for those closest to us in this time together.

If you are not married, pray these things for yourself or your future spouse.
If you are married, pray these specific things for your SPOUSE.

- Walk in integrity, keep promises, and fulfill commitments. (Ps. 15; 112:1-9)
- Be patient, kind, hard to offend, and quick to forgive. (Eph. 4:32; Jas. 1:19)
- Not get distracted or cower into passivity, but embrace responsibility. (Neh. 6:1-4)
- Be surrounded with wise friends and avoid foolish friends. (Prov. 13:20; 1 Cor. 15:33)
- Use good judgment, pursue justice, love mercy, and walk humbly with God. (Mic. 6:8)
- Depend upon God's wisdom and strength rather than own. (Prov. 3:5-6; James 1:5)
- Make choices based upon the fear of God, not the fear of man. (Prov. 9:10; 29:25)
- Break free from any bondage, bad habit, or addiction. (John 8:31, 36; Rom. 6:1-19)
- Find identity and satisfaction in God. (Ps. 37:4; 1 John 2:15-17)
- Read the Word of God and allow it to guide decisions. (Ps.119:105; Matt. 7:24-27)

If you have children, consider praying these things for your CHILDREN.

- That they would be blessed, protected, and prosperous in their role. (3 John 2)
- Submit to the authority and ways of God and His Word daily. (1 Pet. 2:13-17)
- Come to the knowledge of Christ and surrender to His lordship. (1 Tim. 2:4)
- Use good judgment, pursue justice, love mercy, and walk humbly with God. (Mic. 6:8)
- Walk in integrity, keep their promises, and fulfill their commitments. (Ps. 15; 112:1-9)
- Not get distracted or cower into passivity, but embrace responsibility. (Neh. 6:1-14)
- Respect all people without regard to their gender, race, or social status. (1 Pet. 2:17)
- Hate evil, pride, injustice, and turn away from Satan's lies and schemes. (1 Pet. 5:8)
- Become hard workers who faithfully fulfill their duties. (Prov.6:6-11; Luke 12:42-44)
- Make choices based upon the fear of God, not the fear of man. (Prov. 9:10; 29:25)

DAY 2

PRAY FOR THOSE CLOSE TO YOU

In addition to praying for one's family, we also need to discipline ourselves to pray for those we are around on a regular basis.

Paul set a wonderful example for us in his letters of continually praying for groups of people in his sphere of influence. Look up the following verses and make a note beside each about how Paul prayed for that particular group of people.

Philippians 1:3-5

Colossians 1:3

1 Thessalonians 1:2-3

Paul recognized the power of prayer and made it an essential part of his ministry. He knew the needs of those around him and prayed specifically for God to work in their lives according to their current needs.

Are you aware of specific needs of people around you? How can you be intentional this week to learn of particular prayer concerns?

Earlier this week, you heard requests from members of your study group concerning prayer needs. Have you prayed for them yet?

You have passed by coworkers or associates numerous times this week. While you might have talked with them, have you talked with God concerning them?

Read Ephesians 3:14-21 and see how the apostle Paul prayed for the Ephesian church.

What were some of Paul's prayers for the church in Ephesus?

Can you think of anyone in your life that would benefit from a prayer like this?

Let's start getting more detailed. Choose at least one person from your group and one coworker to pray for today.

What are their unique prayer needs? What Bible verses should you pray over them? (Feel free to borrow from Paul's prayer for the Ephesians.) How often should you pray?

After you fill out the chart below, begin to pray for them and watch God at work today. You might even be surprised how much more keen you are to notice God at work in their lives.

Category	Name	Prayer Needs	Verses to Pray	Days to Pray
Person in Your Group				
Coworker				

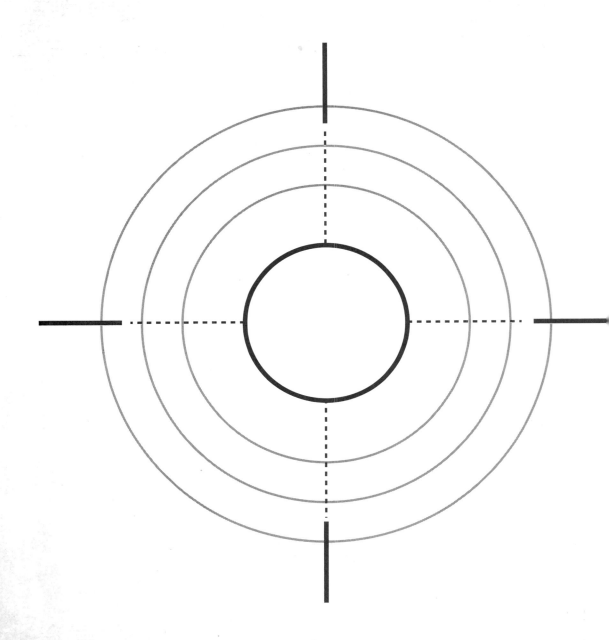

PRAYING FOR OTHER BELIEVERS:

If you haven't already done so, write the names of some other believers in the target to the left. Then use these verses and strategies to pray for them.

- That they would fully surrender their lives to the lordship of Jesus Christ. (Rom. 10:9-10; 12:1-2)

- Grow in Christ and obey the Word of God as a disciple. (John 8:31-32)

- Walk in love, kindness, and favor with the lost and believers around them. (Col. 4:5-6)

- Know the hope, riches, and power of their inheritance in Christ. (Eph. 1:18-19)

- Be devoted to prayer in secret and corporately in the church. (Matt. 6:6; 18:19-20; Col. 4:3)

- Repent of daily sins and walk in holiness before God. (2 Cor. 6:17; Eph. 5:15-18)

- Break free from any bondage, stronghold, or addiction in their lives. (John 8:31, 36; Rom. 6:1-19; 2 Cor. 10:4-5)

- Live with Christ as their hope and true source of peace and happiness. (John 4:10-14)

- Share the gospel and faithfully make disciples of others in their lives. (Matt. 28:18-20)

- Be found faithful when they stand before God. (Matt. 25:21; 1 Tim. 1:12; 2 Tim. 4:7)

DAY 3

PRAY FOR
GOSPEL WORKERS

The Enemy is prowling around like a roaring lion seeking someone to devour (1 Pet. 5:8) and his target is often on those in leadership.

Pastors and ministry leaders pray for many people, but how many people pray for them? We should be thankful for these effective prayers that are lifted up by these gospel workers on our behalf (Jas. 5:16), but we must also not neglect to pray for them in return.

The apostle Paul viewed the Philippian church as a place full of ministers and missionaries for the gospel. In his introductory words to the church in Philippi, he prayed for these gospel workers.

Read Philippians 1:3-11 and circle or underline specific things for which Paul prayed.

3 I thank my God in all my remembrance of you, 4 always offering prayer with joy in my every prayer for you all, 5 in view of your participation in the gospel from the first day until now. 6 For I am confident of this very thing, that He who began a good work in you will perfect it until the day of Christ Jesus. 7 For it is only right for me to feel this way about you all, because I have you in my heart, since both in my imprisonment and in the defense and confirmation of the gospel, you all are partakers of grace with me. 8 For God is my witness, how I long for you all with the affection of Christ Jesus. 9 And this I pray, that your love may abound still more and more in real knowledge and all discernment, 10 so that you may approve the things that are excellent, in order to be sincere and blameless until the day of Christ; 11 having been filled with the fruit of righteousness which comes through Jesus Christ, to the glory and praise of God.

Paul did not pray for these gospel workers out of a sense of obligation. How does he describe his spirit of prayer for them (v. 4)?

We are often tempted to notice the mistakes our church leaders make and focus on what needs to be fixed. Paul prayed specifically that God would complete the good work He started in this church and also that these leaders would be pure and blameless on the day of Christ. This implies that they are not perfect yet, but Paul prayed that God would grow them in their love and knowledge to be more like Him.

Understanding that your own church leaders are not perfect, how can you pray for them according to these verses?

What else did you notice about Paul's prayers for these gospel workers?

It's time to pray for those who pray for others. While these men and women do great things for the kingdom, they are still flesh and blood and tempted and tried like each of us. They need our prayers!

Select at least one church staff member to pray for. Also, select a missionary for whom you can pray. If you don't know one personally, ask your church staff member to give you the name of a missionary as well as prayer needs.

Let's move past vague prayers and generic lists. In this prayer focus, we must do more than just ask simple blessings or safety over categories of ministers and missionaries. Who are these actual people? In what specific ways should you pray for them?

Fill out the chart below completely and get to work praying for these gospel workers today!

Category	Name	Prayer Needs	Verses to Pray	Days to Pray
Church Staff Member				
Missionary				

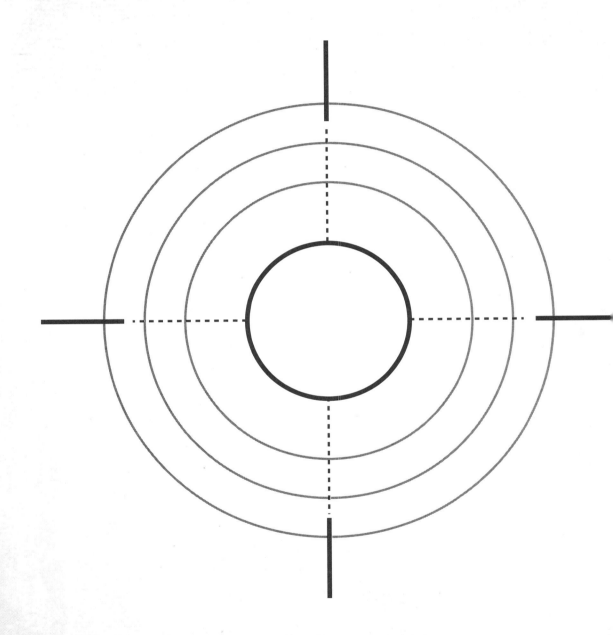

PRAYING FOR YOUR PASTOR/MISSIONARIES:

If you haven't already done so, write the name of your pastor or another minister or missionary in the target to the left. Then pray for them using the Scriptures and requests below.

- That they would love the Lord with all their heart, mind, soul, and strength. (Matt. 22:36-40)

- Honor Christ in heart, words, and actions. (Ps. 19:14; 1 Cor. 11:1; 1 Tim. 1:17; Heb. 5:4)

- Abide in Christ and be devoted to prayer, relying on God. (Acts 1:14; Rom. 12:12; Col. 4:2)

- Rightly divide the Word of truth and communicate the gospel with clarity. (1 Cor. 4:2; Eph. 6:17; 1 Thess. 2:13; 2 Tim. 2:15; 4:2)

- Have a heart for the lost and be an effective and fruitful soul winner. (Mark 16:15; Luke 10:2; 1 Pet. 3:15)

- Provide prayer, encouragement, and resources to undergird their work spiritually and financially. (Isa. 56:7; Phil. 4:18-19)

- Help them serve in the power of God's Spirit and not in the flesh. (John 15:4-10; Gal. 5:16-25; 1 John 2:20, 27)

- Walk in purity and be protected from the deceptive schemes of Satan. (Eph. 4:27; 2 Thess. 3:3; 1 Tim. 3:7; Jas. 4:7; 1 Pet. 5:8)

- Grant them good health, rest, and refreshment from the Lord. (Ex. 33:14; Matt. 11:28; 3 John 2)

- Bless them with strong marriages and families amid the hard work of ministry. (Eph. 5:22–6:4; 1 Tim. 3:4-5)

PRAY FOR THOSE NEGLECTED

While we have gladly spent time praying for family, friends, coworkers, and gospel workers, the Bible commands us to pray for another group of people—those often neglected. It may not be the type of "neglect" that comes to your mind. These people aren't neglected by a world's standard but from a prayer standard.

Who are these people? Politicians and persecutors.

Throughout the Bible, God singles out these two groups of people and expects and commands our prayers for them.

Read the passages below and answer the questions that follow.

First of all, then, I urge that entreaties and prayers, petitions and thanksgivings, be made on behalf of all men, 2 for kings and all who are in authority, so that we may lead a tranquil and quiet life in all godliness and dignity.
1 TIMOTHY 2:1-2

But I say to you, love your enemies and pray for those who persecute you.
MATTHEW 5:44

What makes it difficult to pray for politicians and those in authority?

Instead of praying for those who persecute you, how do you naturally want to respond to them?

According to 1 Timothy 2:1-2, what benefit do we receive in praying for those in authority?

Again we can look to Jesus' example on this tough subject. Jesus used some of His final breaths on the cross to pray for His own persecutors who reviled and mocked Him.

> *But Jesus was saying, "Father, forgive them; for they do not know what they are doing." And they cast lots, dividing up His garments among themselves.*
> **LUKE 23:34**

What words would you use to describe Jesus' prayer for His persecutors?

In this moment, do you think Jesus expects anything in return from them?

Jesus' prayer is selfless. His prayer is not intended to change their actions for His own gain, but simply to plead to the Father on their behalf.

While this day's prayer focus may not be the list you are most eager to begin, it is a clear biblical command. That's why we must address it. Select at least one politician or person in authority for whom you can pray. It may not even be one that you respect or like. Even if they think fundamentally different than your side of the ticket, wouldn't you desire to see God still do a work in their lives?

It may be difficult for you to think of an enemy or persecutor in your life. For some of you, it might be easy. Who is that person who makes you cringe when you see them from far off or hear their name mentioned? That person might be a good place to start. Pray in the Spirit and not in the flesh. Don't just pray that God will "get them," but pray that God works in their lives.

This day's assignment is important to the whole process. We are submitting ourselves to the teaching of Scripture and we cannot neglect such clear commands. Let's become obedient to the Word and get to praying!

Category	Name	Prayer Needs	Verses to Pray	Days to Pray
Politician (1 Tim. 2:2)				
Persecutor (Matt. 5:44)				

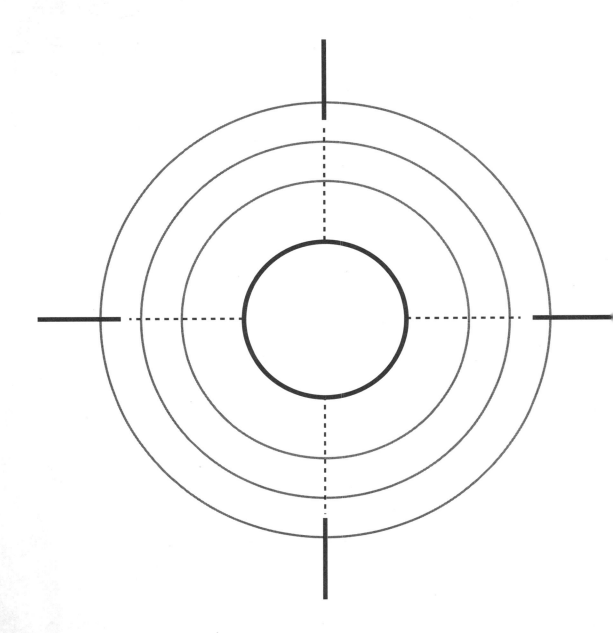

CONSIDER PRAYING THE FOLLOWING PRAYERS FOR YOUR THOSE IN AUTHORITY:

If you haven't already done so, write the names of government, work, or family authorities in the target to the left. Then use the Scriptures and strategies below to pray for them.

- That they would be blessed, protected, and prosperous in their role. (3 John 2)

- Lead with honor, respect, wisdom, compassion, and godliness. (1 Tim. 2:2)

- Watch over, protect, lead, and serve those in their care. (Heb. 13:17)

- Come to the knowledge of Christ and surrender to His lordship. (1 Tim. 2:4)

- Establish rules and laws that honor God's law and strengthen families and cities. (Deut. 10:13)

- Submit to the authority and ways of God and His Word daily. (1 Pet. 2:13-17)

- Hate evil, pride, injustice, and turn away from Satan's lies and schemes. (1 Pet. 5:8)

- Become hard workers who faithfully fulfill their duties. (Prov. 6:6-11; Luke 12:42-44)

- Use good judgment, pursue justice, love mercy, and walk humbly with God. (Mic. 6:8)

- Be a godly example in their roles and responsibilities. (Josh. 24:15)

PRAY FOR THOSE IN NEED

Oftentimes, prayer lists in churches are full of those in need. It is very normal to pray for those who have medical setbacks, personal loss, and situations of grief. In these moments, the lists can grow very long and the prayer time can unfortunately grow very short.

Think of all the legitimate needs around you. Instead of letting them overwhelm you, begin to pray for them!

How would God want you to pray for someone who is going through a difficult time?

Read 2 Corinthians 1:8-11 and note key phrases that can aid you in your prayers just as the church in Corinth prayed for Paul in his afflictions.

8 For we do not want you to be unaware, brethren, of our affliction which came to us in Asia, that we were burdened excessively, beyond our strength, so that we despaired even of life; 9 indeed, we had the sentence of death within ourselves so that we would not trust in ourselves, but in God who raises the dead; 10 who delivered us from so great a peril of death, and will deliver us, He on whom we have set our hope. And He will yet deliver us, 11 you also joining in helping us through your prayers, so that thanks may be given by many persons on our behalf for the favor bestowed on us through the prayers of many.
2 CORINTHIANS 1:8-11

What about those who have the greatest need of all—a spiritual one? How should we pray for someone who doesn't know Jesus?

Read Ephesians 1:17-19 and underline key words in Paul's prayer.

17 I pray that the God of our Lord Jesus Christ, the glorious Father, would give you a spirit of wisdom and revelation in the knowledge of Him. 18 I pray that the perception of your mind may be enlightened so you may know what is the hope of His calling, what are the glorious riches of His inheritance among the saints, 19 and what is the immeasurable greatness of His power to us who believe, according to the working of His vast strength.
EPHESIANS 1:17-19, HCSB

With needs so great, we cannot rely on our own power to remedy such situations. We must rely on the power of God. As we plead with Him in prayer, we expect great things from Him because we know that He is able to do even more than what we could ask from Him (Eph. 3:20).

Select at least one person for each of the categories below. Get specific in the prayer needs, verses to pray, and how often to pray. In addition to praying for these people, today you could make contact and let them know that you prayed for them.

For the person in need, a simple message telling him or her that you prayed and a verse you prayed would serve as a huge encouragement.

For the person who doesn't know Jesus, a simple message saying that you had him or her on your mind and wanted to know if there was something for which you could pray could open up some doors to the gospel.

Category	Name	Prayer Needs	Verses to Pray	Days to Pray
Person in Need				
Lost Person				

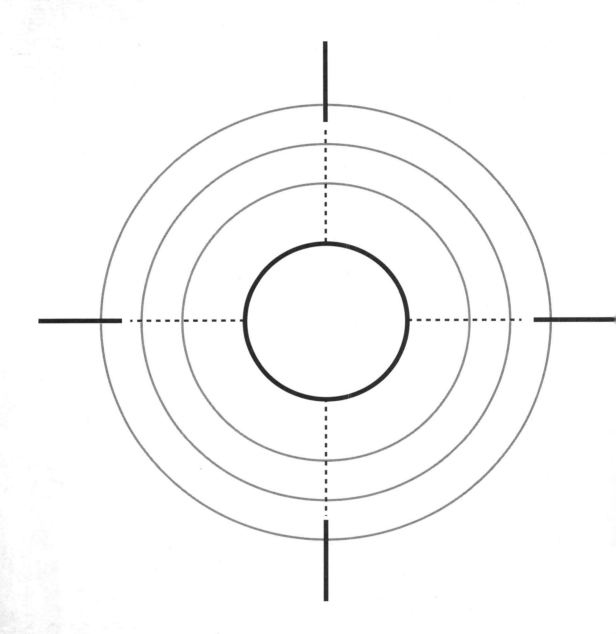

PRAYING FOR THE LOST:

If you haven't already done so, write the names of lost family or friends in the target to the left. Then use the Scriptures and strategies below to pray specifically for them.

- That God would connect them to genuine believers and the simplicity of the gospel. (Rom. 1:16; 1 Tim. 2:5-6)

- Disconnect them from influences that are pulling them away from Christ. (John 7:47-52)

- Expose the lies they've believed that have kept them from Christ. (2 Cor. 4:4)

- Show mercy, bind Satan, and turn them from darkness to light so they may receive forgiveness of sins. (Luke 19:10; Acts 26:18)

- Convict them of sin, God's coming judgment, and their need for a Savior. (John 3:18; 16:8-9; 1 Cor. 1:18; Eph. 2:1)

- Save them, change their hearts, and fill them with God's Spirit. (Ezek. 36:26; John 3:16; Eph. 5:18)

- Help them be baptized and get plugged into a Bible-teaching church. (Matt. 28:18-20)

- Help them live with Christ as their hope and true source of peace and happiness. (John 4:10-14)

- Deliver them from evil, the devil's traps and schemes, and any strongholds. (2 Cor. 10:4-5)

- Help them abide in Christ and live according to His will. (John 15:1-17)

We hope that the strategy for prayer that you have been building over these last eight weeks will guide your prayer life for the future. Feel free to download copies of the Prayer Strategy Target at *www.LifeWay.com/BattlePlan* and use them to pray for others.

May the Lord bless you and keep you as you follow after Him in all the areas of your life.

VIDEO CONTRIBUTORS

We would like to thank these amazing servants of God for sharing advice and their experiences through prayer in the video teaching sessions of *Battle Plan for Prayer*. Video teaching sessions available for purchase at *LifeWay.com/BattlePlan*.

CLAUDE KING serves as Discipleship & Church Health Specialist at LifeWay Christian Resources. He is author or coauthor of numerous books and discipleship courses including *Experiencing God, The Mind of Christ, The Call to Follow Christ, Growing Disciples: Pray in Faith,* and *Concentric Circles of Concern*. Claude serves as President of the Board of Directors for Final Command Ministries.

KAY HORNER serves as Executive Director for the Center for Spiritual Renewal and Awakening America Alliance and the National Coordinator for the Cry Out America prayer initiative with the Alliance and has been chosen as a member of the National Prayer Committee and Mission America Coalition/U.S. Lausanne Committee.

DAVE BUTTS is a conference speaker and serves on several Boards of Directors and committees focused on prayer, revival, and evangelism including America's National Prayer Committee. In 1993 Dave and his wife, Kim, launched Harvest Prayer Ministries. Dave is the author of several books, including *When God Shows Up,*
Desperate for Change, Prayer and the End of Days, Revolution on Our Knees, and *Pray Like the King.*

P. DOUGLAS SMALL is President and Founder of Alive Ministries: PROJECT PRAY, an organization he has led for more than 25 years. He is an Ordained Bishop and the International Coordinator for Prayer Ministries for the Church of God denomination. He also serves as a member of the National Prayer Committee and on the leadership team of the Denominational Prayer Committee. He is the prayer consultant to the Billion Souls Campaign initiative.

GLENN SHEPPARD, along with his wife Jacquelyn, co-founded International Prayer Ministries, Inc. Prior to the beginning of International Prayer Ministries in 1986, he pioneered the Office of Prayer and Spiritual Awakening for the North American Mission Board of the Southern Baptist Convention for almost eight years.

PRISCILLA SHIRER is a wife and mom, a speaker and author of several books and Bible studies, including *Fervent* and *The Armor of God Bible Study*. Through Going Beyond Ministries, she and her husband Jerry count it as their privilege to minister to people from all cultures and denominations.

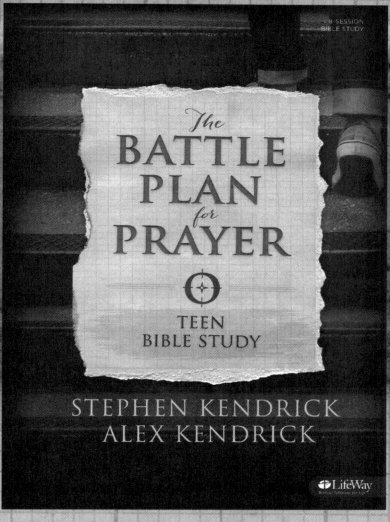

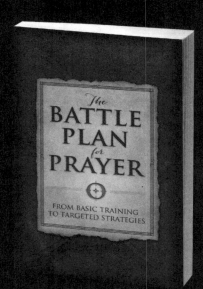